# THE BEST OF
# PUNCH
## CARTOONS

ACKNOWLEDGEMENT

This book could not have been completed without the input and assistance of
the team at Punch Cartoon Library: Andre Gailani, Brian Moss, Nick Roberts

This edition published in 2017
First published in Great Britain in 2008 by Prion
an imprint of
The Carlton Publishing Group
20 Mortimer Street
London W1T 3JW

10 9 8 7 6 5

A catalogue record for this book is available from the British Library

ISBN 978-1-85375-996-3

Editorial Manager: Roland Hall
Design: Anna Pow & Paul Chattaway
Production: Claire Hayward

Printed in China

*Above*: cartoon by Richard Doyle.

*Opposite*: cartoon by Charles Keene.

*Previous page*: cartoon by E H Shepard.

*Contents pages, top left*: cartoon by William Hewison;
 *bottom right*: cartoon by Norman Mansbridge.

# THE BEST OF
# PUNCH
# CARTOONS

"Toots! there's no a Jok i' th' 'hale beuk!"

EDITED BY
## HELEN WALASEK

## 2,000 Classic illustrations

PRION

# CONTENTS

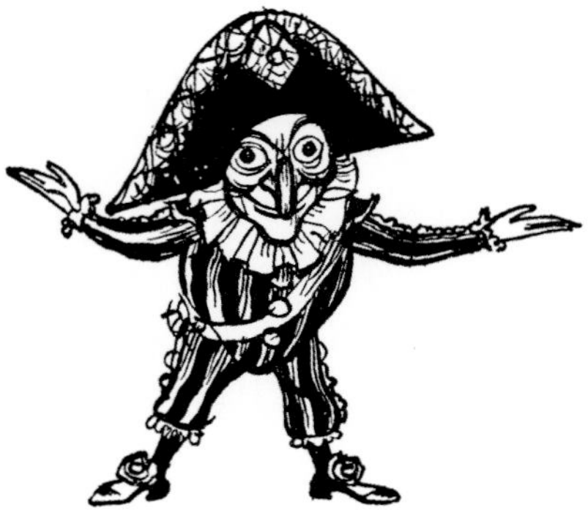

# FOREWORD

## MOHAMED AL FAYED

### CHAIRMAN OF PUNCH LIMITED

**P**unch is a national treasure, a British institution that amused generations of readers throughout the nineteenth and twentieth centuries – and into the twenty-first. Its long and rich heritage of humour is perhaps best represented by the thousands of incomparable cartoons printed in its pages over 160 years. *The Best of Punch Cartoons* is the largest selection of *Punch* cartoons ever published and gives a wonderful flavour of the many fascinating treasures that can be found in the magazine's cartoon archive. It brings these old favourites back to their many enthusiastic admirers and introduces them to a new generation of fans.

I was immensely proud when I acquired *Punch* and was able to revive it in 1996, and I am pleased now to be able to commend to you this magnificent book with its superb collection of some of the greatest *Punch* cartoons.

**Mohamed Al Fayed**

*Opposite*: The cover of *Punch* designed by Richard Doyle in 1849 and used for the next 107 years until colour covers were introduced in the 1950s.

PUNCH

No. 391. VOLUME THE SIXTEENTH. JANUARY 6, 1849.

PUBLISHED EVERY SATURDAY.

PRICE THREEPENCE. STAMPED, 4d.

PUNCH OFFICE, 85, FLEET STREET.
AND SOLD BY ALL BOOKSELLERS AND NEWSMEN.

# INTRODUCTION

## Helen Walasek

A very British institution for over 160 years, *Punch* was the world's most celebrated magazine of humour and satire – imitated, parodied and pirated (but never bettered) from America to Japan. It played a starring role in Britain's idea of itself – and how the rest of the world saw the British. *Punch* published some of the finest comic writers in the English language from William Thackeray to P G Wodehouse and Alan Coren, while its legendary political cartoons by giants like Tenniel and Partridge swayed the governments of the day. Scattered through its pages, like tasty plums in a pudding, were witty cartoons from the pens of the great: Leech, du Maurier, Phil May, H M Bateman, Pont, E H Shepard, Fougasse, Emett,

Anton, Thelwell, Searle, Heath…

From the leather-bound volumes resting on the shelves of aristocratic libraries, to the issues read in suburban sitting-rooms and club-houses in the most distant territories of the Empire, *Punch* touched a wide swathe of British society. But the magazine ascended to much airier realms: dining with Czar Alexander II in 1876, a surprised British Ambassador was handed a copy of *Punch* by the Czar opened at Tenniel's cartoon *A Break in the Game* – in which Alexander appeared to be cheating at cards. "Expliquez-moi cela" demanded the Czar. After a tactical pause, the ambassador offered a more diplomatic interpretation of the cartoon.

CARTOON, N°. I.

SUBSTANCE AND SHADOW.

*Above*: *Substance and Shadow*, John Leech's famous *Cartoon No. 1* of 1843 mocking the government's costly exhibition of preliminary sketches for wall paintings to decorate the new Houses of Parliament while Londoners starved. This was the first use of the word 'cartoon' for a satirical drawing and the name stuck.

*Opposite*: The first cover of *Punch* by Archibald Henning.

LONDON:
PUBLISHED FOR THE PROPRIETORS, BY R. BRYANT,
AT PUNCH'S OFFICE, WELLINGTON STREET, STRAND.
AND SOLD BY ALL BOOKSELLERS.

**UNDER THE CENSOR'S STAMP;**
Or, how the Bear's Paw comes down on *Punch* in St. Petersburg. And yet the Jingoes call him "Russophil"!

*Punch* was born in the ferment of early Victorian publishing where periodicals quickly appeared (and just as quickly disappeared), produced by a shifting group of journalists, writers, printers and engravers who drank in the same pubs and ate at the same eating houses. Punch was no exception. One such pub was (appropriately enough) the Shakespeare's Head, kept by *Punch's* future editor, Mark Lemon. The founders of the new magazine were the wood engraver Ebenezer Landells and writer Henry Mayhew, along with three other shareholders including Lemon. As for the magazine's name, the legend went that someone remarked the new paper should be like a good mixture of *Punch* – nothing without Lemon – to which Mayhew cried: 'A capital idea! We'll call it Punch!' and a prospectus was drawn up announcing 'A new work of wit and whim embellished with cuts and caricatures'.

On July 17, 1841 the first issue of *Punch* appeared, with a cover drawn by Archibald Henning. After a wobbly start the magazine began to establish itself, particularly after the introduction of the first Almanack for 1842 when circulation shot up. *Punch* had found a gap in the market that was waiting to be filled – the lurid sensationalism of the contemporary comic press was no longer acceptable in the sedate drawing rooms of the growing Victorian middle classes and Punch aimed to be humorous without being vulgar. It quickly gathered a corps of some of the era's literary stars like Thackeray and Douglas Jerrold and artists such as John Leech and Richard 'Dicky' Doyle. By the end of 1842 all the shares in the magazine had been bought by the publishers and printers Bradbury & Evans, later Bradbury & Agnew, who were to be *Punch's* proprietors until 1969.

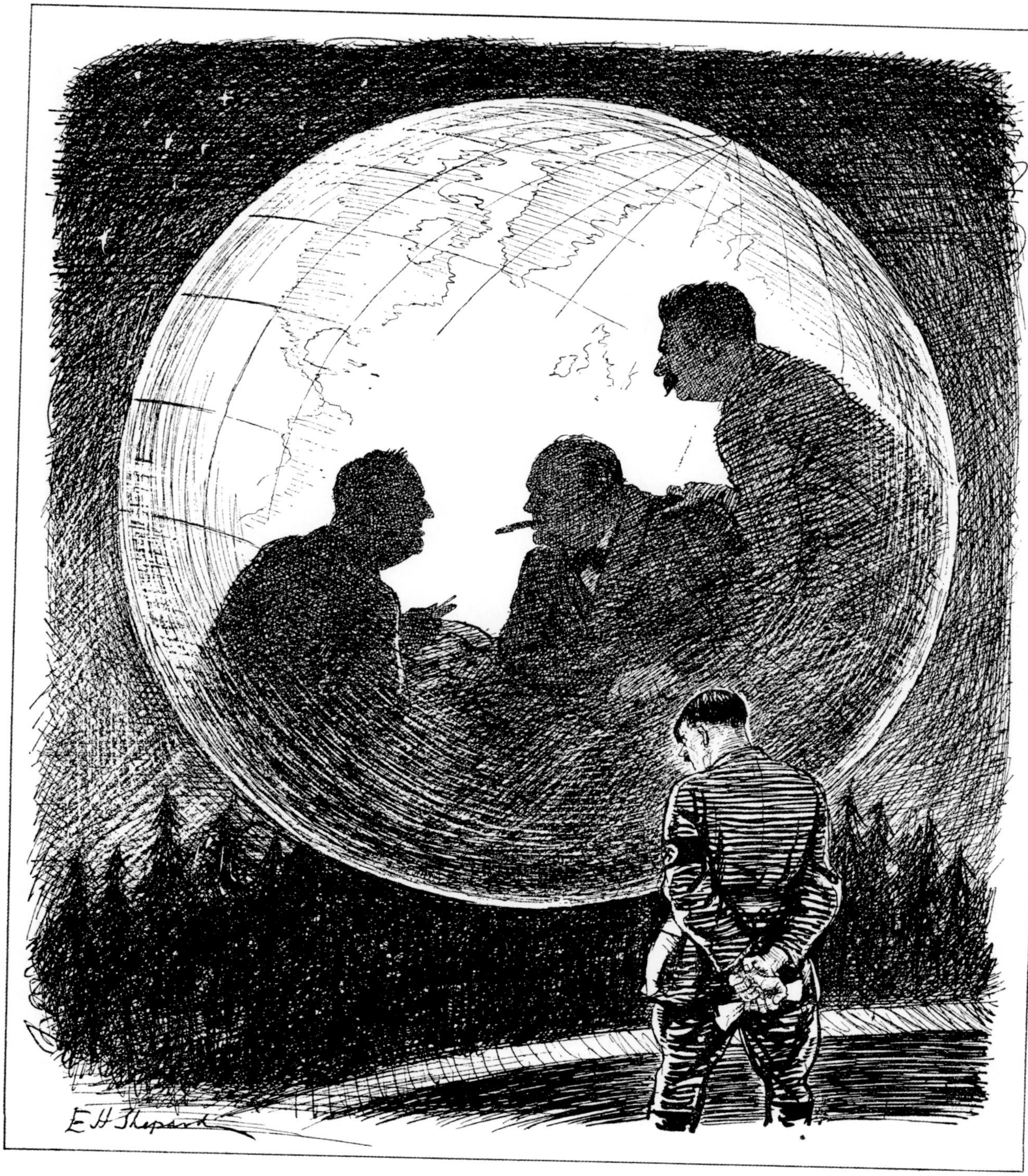
E H Shepard

THE FATES DECIDE.

Linley Sambourne, 1891

"THE MAHOGANY TREE."

*Punch's* cover went through six incarnations before the final classic design by Richard Doyle was settled on in January 1849 with its twiggy elf-infested masthead and the magazine's alter-ego: Mr Punch and his dog Toby. It was to remain unchanged for 107 years when colour covers were introduced. Two other long-running traditions were the *Punch* Dinners and the *Punch* Table – this last was both a real table and an exclusive club. The ritual of the editor, proprietor, staff and contributors discussing the coming issue and the subject of the Big Cut (the large political cartoon) over a convivial meal began soon after the magazine's foundation and the famous table (now in the British Library)

purchased early in *Punch's* history. Christened 'The Mahogany Tree' by Thackeray, but in reality a rather unremarkable table of cheap deal (grandly banded in oak by Ambrose Heal in 1930), it is a legendary artefact of the British literary scene. The table's surface is engraved with scores of initials – those of *Punch's* editors at one end, its proprietors' at the other, while ranged along the sides are those of a select band of some of the nineteenth and twentieth centuries' greatest illustrators and writers. As for becoming a member of the Table, it was not enough simply to contribute to the magazine – the coveted membership was by invitation only.

At the start *Punch* had radical ideas of social justice, unafraid to be a thorn in the side of the powers that be. As the decades passed and the magazine achieved its apotheosis as National Institution, it aligned itself increasingly with the upper ranks of society. By the turn of the twentieth century two successive editors, Francis Burnand and Owen Seaman, were given knighthoods along with its chief political cartoonists, John Tenniel and Bernard Partridge. *Punch* had become a fully paid-up member of the Establishment. After the Great War *Punch* was called 'a magazine produced by schoolmasters for schoolmasters' – but this was squarely in tune with the interests of the suburban middle classes, and ever more copies were sold. Now readers were laughing at cartoons by Bateman, Fougasse and Pont. During WWII, *Punch* was considered so essential to Home Front morale its publishers were given extra allocations of paper.

*Punch* continued to be a national icon well into the post-war era. Circulation rose to an all-time high, and cartoons like Russell Brockbank's sporty cars embodied a growing optimism. In the 1960s and 1970s the magazine acquired a new bite and a fresh generation of cartoonists such as ffolkes, Heath, Honeysett and Mike Williams were nurtured, leading to a golden age of cartooning in the 1980s and early 1990s. But after the departure of much-loved editor Alan Coren in 1987 and a dwindling circulation, the writing was on the wall and on

- 13 -

April 8, 1992 *Punch* ceased publication. Re-launched in 1996, the magazine again became a gadfly of the Establishment; but times had changed, *Punch* was unable to re-establish itself and closed in 2002.

The legend of *Punch's* cartoons lives on, and this book offers a bumper crop of the best, from the exquisite aristocratic satires of du Maurier to the outrageous gags of Husband and Banx – the rude boys of the 1990s – who, with the sex, drugs and rock-and-roll of the 1960s' and 1970s' cartoonists, lifted *Punch's* cartoons far away from the careful blandness of *The New Yorker's*. *Punch* printed some of the most celebrated cartoons ever published – immortals like du Maurier's *True Humility* (better known as *The Curate's Egg*), Paul Crum's 'I keep thinking it's Tuesday', Sillince's harried businessman and his tranquil gardener, and Birkett's bumbling Daleks, alongside series like H M Bateman's *The Man Who...*, Pont's *The British Character*, Thelwell's ponies, Searle's *The Rake's Progress*, and Handelsman's *Freaky Fables*. You'll find them all in this feast of humour and artistry – a portrait of the British seen through the beady and observant eyes of *Punch's* cartoonists and the funniest book you'll read this decade.

**Helen Walasek** works at *Punch* Cartoon Library and is former curator of the *Punch* Archive and Collection.

*Left*: *Punch* staff seated round the Punch Table toast Mr Punch on the magazine's 50th anniversary led by editor Francis Burnand, with chief cartoonist John Tenniel seated to his left.

*Above*: Versions of Mr. Punch drawn for the magazine's 120th anniversary in 1961, from left to right, by Quentin Blake, Smilby, Fougasse and Norman Thelwell.

# 1841–1913
## VICTORIANS AND EDWARDIANS

John Leech, 1845

**'PARTIES' FOR THE GALLOWS**

*Newsvender:* 'Now, my man, what is it?' *Boy:* 'I vonts a nillustrated newspaper with a norrid murder and a likeness in it.'

John Leech, 1850

**A DROP OF LONDON WATER.**

John Leech, 1848

*Affectionate Husband*: 'Come, Polly - if I am a little irritable, it's over in a minute!'

AQUARIUS. PISCES.

JANUARY——FEBRUARY.

Innocent Mirth——The Slide on the Pavement.

General Thaw, and Bursting of the Water-pipes.

Richard Doyle & John Leech, 1848

Richard Doyle, 1849

A. VIEW OF Mʳ LORDE hys CRYKET GROVNDE.

John Leech, 1856

John Tenniel, 1851

**A NICE BRACING DAY AT THE SEA-SIDE**

# BROWN, JONES, AND ROBINSON GO TO THE ZOOLOGICAL GARDENS.

THEY INSPECT THE BEARS.

ROBINSON FEEDS THE WATER-FOWL.

BROWN HAVING RASHLY STRAYED INTO A ROOM FULL OF MACAWS,
WE SEE THE CONSEQUENCE.

JONES VOLUNTEERS TO RIDE THE CAMEL, AND, TO A CERTAIN EXTENT,
HE DOES IT.

IN A LONELY PATHWAY THEY SEE SOMETHING COMING.

THEY ARE PERSUADED TO MOUNT THE ELEPHANT.

THEY GO IN QUEST OF THE HIPPOPOTAMUS.

THEY SEE THE HIPPOPOTAMUS!

Richard Doyle, 1850

William Makepeace Thackeray, 1848

John Leech, 1854

### AUTHORS' MISERIES. NO VI.

*Old gentleman. Miss Wiggets. Two authors.*
*Old gentleman.* 'I am sorry to see you occupied, My dear Miss Wiggets,
with that trivial paper 'Punch.' A railway is not a place, in my opinion,
for jokes. I never joke—never.'
*Miss W.* 'So I should think, sir.'
*Old gentleman.* 'And besides, are you aware who are the conductors of
that paper, and that they are Chartists, Deists, Atheists, Anarchists, and
Socialists, to a man? I have it from the best authority, that they meet
together once a week in a tavern in Saint Giles's, where they concoct their
infamous print. The chief part of their income is derived from threatening
letters which they send to the nobility and gentry. The principal writer is a
returned convict. Two have been tried at the Old Bailey; And their artist—as
for their artist... *Guard:* 'Swin-dun! Sta-tion!' [*Exeunt two authors*.]

### FURTHER ILLUSTRATION OF
### THE MINING DISTRICTS

*First Polite Native.* 'Who's 'im, Bill?'
*Second ditto.* ' A stranger!'
*First ditto.* ''Eave 'arf a brick at 'im.'

John Leech, 1852

### ALARMING!

*Hairdresser.* 'They say, sir, the cholera's in the hair, sir!'
*Gent, very uneasy.* 'Indeed! Ahem! Then I hope you're very particular about the brushes you use.'
*Hairdresser.* 'Oh! I see you don't hunderstand me, sir. I don't mean the 'air of the 'ed, but the hair hof the hatomsphere!'

*(Heading for Volume 27 showing Punch staff at play)*

John Tenniel, 1854

Richard Doyle, 1849

John Leech, 1852

**GRAND SHOW OF PRIZE VEGETARIANS**

# JOHN LEECH 1817-1864

Leech joined the fledgling *Punch* team in August 1841 and soon became its star turn, his prolific and fluid pen dashing off acerbic political cartoons and witty 'socials' with equal skill. Praised by John Ruskin for his gentle but acute observations of all classes of society, Leech's *Pictures of Life and Character* epitomised mid-Victorian England. As his old friend William Thackeray cried in 1854: "Fancy a number of *Punch* without Leech's pictures! What would you give for it?"

John Leech, 1848

**FLUNKIANA**

*Enter Thomas, who gives warning.*
*Gentlemen:* 'Oh, certainly! You can go, of course; But, as you have been with me for nine years, I should like to know the reason.'
*Thomas:* 'Why, sir, it's my feelins. You used always to read prayers, sir, yourself—and since Miss Wilkins has bin here, she bin a reading of 'em.  Now I can't  bemean myself sayin 'Amen' to a guv'ness.'

John Leech, 1853

**A STARTLING NOVELTY IN SHIRTS**

John Leech, 1854

*New cricketing dresses, to protect All England against the present swift bowling*

John Leech, 1852

John Leech, 1852

*Railway official.* 'You'd better not smoke, sir!'
*Traveller.* 'That's what my friends say.'
*Railway official.* 'But you mustn't smoke, sir!'
*Traveller.* 'So my doctor tells me.'
*Railway official (indignantly).* 'But you shan't smoke, sir!'
*Traveller.* 'Ah! Just what my wife says.'

**PLEASANT!**
*Nervous gentleman.* 'Don't you think, Robert, going so
fast down hill, is very likely to make the horse fall?'
*Robert.* 'Lor bless yer—no, sir! I never throwed a oss down in my life,
'xcept once; and that was one frosty moonlight night (just such a night
as this it was), as I was a-drivin' a gent (as might be you) from the station
when I throwed down this werry oss, in this werry identical place!'

John Leech, 1852

**ROMANCE AND REALITY**
*Beautiful being (who is all soul).* 'How grand, how solemn, dear Frederick, this is! I really think the Ocean is more beautiful
under this aspect than under any other!'
*Frederick (who has about as much poetry in him as a codfish.* 'Hm—Ah! Yes. Per-waps. By the way, Blanche—There's a
fella shwimping. S'pose we ask him if he can get us some pwawns for bweakfast, to-morwaw morning?'

A·RAYLWAY·STATYON·   SHOWYNGE Yᵉ TRAVELLERS·REFRESHYNGE·THEMSELVES·

Richard Doyle, 1849

John Leech, 1852

**RAILWAY LITERATURE**
*Book-stall keeper.* 'Book, ma'am? Yes, ma'am. Here's
a popular work by an eminent surgeon, just published.
'Broken Legs: And How to Mend Them;' or, would you
like the last number of 'The Railway Operator?"

John Leech, 1852

**AN AFFAIR OF IMPORTANCE**
*Harriet.* 'Oh! I'm so glad you are come, Blanche! I have
been so perplexed I could hardly sleep all night.'
*Blanche.* 'Well! What is it, dear?' *Harriet.* 'Why, I don't know
whether to have my new merino frock violet or dark blue!'

John Leech, 1860

*Cabby.* 'You've no call to git out, sir! He's only a little okard at startin!'

John Leech, 1853

*First Cock Sparrow.* 'What a miwackulous tye, Fwank.
How the doose do you manage it?'
*Second Cock Sparrow.* 'Yas. I fancy it is rather grand; but then,
you see, I give the whole of my mind to it!'

John Leech, 1852

**HORRIBLE INCIDENT IN REAL LIFE**
*As the servants are gone to bed, the master of the house endeavours to get a little bit of supper
for himself. He can't conceive where the deuce the things are all kept; And he is almost torn
to pieces by the black natives of the kitchen. [It may be urged that the natives, as represented
in the tableau, are small in proportion to the other objects; but, as they are not agreeable
creatures, it was thought advisable to keep them down in size.]*

# THE GREAT EXHIBITION
## OF 1851

O ver six million people streamed into London for the Great Exhibition of 1851, first and most renowned of the huge world fairs of the late nineteenth century. It was *Punch* that had christened the exhibition's glittering glass structure 'The Crystal Palace' and its cartoons both celebrated and satirised the momentous event. The introduction of 'shilling days' so working class visitors could attend the fair had excited bourgeois fears of social disorder – *The Pound and the Shilling* records the peaceful (and unlikely) mixing of different classes in its crowded halls.

John Leech, 1851

**CROWDED STATE OF LODGING HOUSES**
*Lodging-housekeeper.* 'On'y this room to let, mem. A four-post—a tent—and a very comfortable double-bedded chest of drawers for the young gentleman.'

John Leech, 1851

**THE GREAT EXHIBITION -
THE DIVING-DRESS DEPARTMENT**
In the foreground is a troublesome boy (who has strayed from his party) and come suddenly upon the figure. He is hurrying away – fear depicted on his countenance.

**KEY TO TABLEAU**
1, Diving-Dress complete.
2, A Troublesome Boy.
3, 4, 5, 6, His Party.

John Leech, 1851

**LONDON DINING ROOMS, 1851**
*Waiter (to Chinaman).* 'Very nice birds'-nest soup, sir!—Yes, sir!—Rat pie, sir, just up.—Yes, sir!—And a nice little dog to foller—yes, sir!'

John Tenniel, 1851

**SCENE—A GREENGROCER'S SHOP, LONDON.**
*Dramatis personae—Greengrocer, and old lady.*
*Old lady—(holding a very small cabbage)—loquitur*: 'What! 3d.
for such a small cabbage? Why, I never heerd o' such a thing!'
*Greengrocer*: 'Werry sorry, marm; But it's all along o' that exhibition!
What with them foreigners, and the gents as smokes, cabbages has riz.'

John Leech, 1851

**THE POUND AND THE SHILLING**
'Whoever Thought of Meeting You Here?'

John Leech, 1854

**ROTTEN ROW IN 1851.**

**PERFECTLY DWEADFUL**

*Guard.* 'Now, sir! If you're going on by express. Here's just room for one!'
*Tourist.* 'Wha-t! Get in with hawwid old women, and squeeming children! By
jove! You know! I say! It's impawsible, you know!'

John Leech, 1857

**A SUBURBAN DELIGHT**

*Dark party (with a ticket-of-leave, of course).* 'Ax yer pardon, sir!—But if you
was a-goin down this dark lane, p'raps you'd allow me and this here
young man to go along with yer—'cos yer see there hain't no perlice
about—and we're so precious feared o' bein' garotted!'

- 26 -

John Leech, 1857

**ART-PROGRESS**

*Artist (!)* 'Now, Mum! Take orf yer 'ead for
sixpence, or yer 'ole body for a shillin' !'

John Leech, 1859

**HUSBAND-TAMING**

John Leech, 1856

**LIFE IN AN AMERICAN HOTEL?**

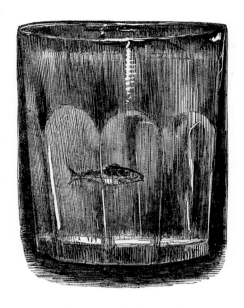

John Leech, 1850

Mr Briggs tries (for many hours) a likely place for a perch;
But, upon this occasion, the wind is not in a favourable quarter.

Minnow caught by Mr Briggs,
August 23rd, 1850.—
Exact size of life.

- 27

John Leech, 1855

'Well, Jack! Here's good news from home. We're to have a medal.'
'That's very kind. Maybe one of these days we'll have a coat to stick it on?'

George du Maurier, 1895

Charles Keene, 1868

**A HOME TRUTH**

*Host (sotto voce).* 'Is this the best claret, Mary?'
*Mary (audibly).* 'It's the best you've got, sir!'

**THRIFT**

*Peebles body (to townsman who was supposed to be in London
on a visit).* 'E—eh, Mac! Ye're sune hame again!'
*Mac.* 'E—eh, it's just a ruinous place, that! Mun, a had na' been
the-erre abune twa hoours when—bang—went saxpence!!!'

Charles Keene, 1867

**COLLOQUIAL EQUIVALENTS**

*Papa.* 'Now, my dear girls, your brother is receiving a most expensive education, and I think that
while he is at home for the holidays you should try to learn something from him.'
*Emily.* 'So we do, 'Pa. We've learnt that a boy who cries is a 'Blub,' that a boy who works hard is
a 'Swot''— *Flora.* 'Yes, and that anybody you don't like is a 'Cad;' and we know the meaning of
'Grub,' 'Prog,' and a 'Wax!''

George du Maurier, 1869

**TO SUFFERERS FROM NERVOUS DEPRESSION.**

*It's very well to go down for six weeks into the country by yourself, to give up tobacco and stimulants, and to live the whole day, so to speak, in the open air; But all this will do you no good, unless you cultivate a cheerful frame of mind, and take a lively view of things.*

George du Maurier, 1870

**OUR COUNTRYMEN ABROAD**
*Sketch of a bench on the boulevards, occupied by four English people who only know each other by sight.*

George du Maurier, 1888

**THINGS ONE WOULD RATHER HAVE LEFT UNSAID**

*Aunt Jane.* 'Ugh! When I was your age, Matilda, ladies of rank and position didn't have their photographs exposed in the shop-windows.'
*Matilda (always anxious to agree).* 'Of course not, Aunt Jane. I suppose photography wasn't invented then?'

# CHARLES KEENE
## 1823-1891

Called "the greatest English artist since Hogarth" by Whistler, collected by Degas and praised by Pissarro, one of the great mysteries of the Victorian art scene is why Charles Keene never became a household name. His superb drawings taxed the skills of the wood block engravers who heroically tried to reproduce his complex lines. But jokes were never Keene's forté and he often resorted to using gags provided by friends like Joseph Crawhall Sr, father of the painter Joseph Crawhall.

Charles Keene, 1874

**A SCHOOL-BOARD PERPLEXITY**
*Active member (to mother of numerous 'irregulars' and 'absentees').* 'Joseph is just turned thirteen, and therefore 'clear;' Simon, you tell us, is sickening for the measles, and Mary is gone into the country to nurse her aunt's baby. What have you to say respecting Peter and James?'
*Mother (of 'irregulars' and 'absentees').* 'Please, sir, they be twins. Can't you allow 'em as one, and let 'em do half a day each?'
*[Active member is puzzled. Orders mother to stand aside, and requests clerk to refer to Mr Forster's Act 'for law bearing on point.'*

Charles Keene, 1871

**'MANNERS.'**
*Pedestrian (blandly).* 'Could you direct me the nearest way to South Kensington?' *Cabman (who sees at a glance the party does not 'mean business').* 'If you wants to be druv there, I'm bound to take yer. Otherwise, I'm not bound to supply general information to the public.'

Charles Keene, 1876

**'THE MEAT SUPPLY.'**
*Bathing-Man.* 'Yes, Mum, he's a good old 'orse yet. And he's been in the salt water so long, he'll make capital biled beef when we're done with him!!!'

## A PANIC IN THE KITCHEN

*Facetious Page*. 'Now, then, here's the Census, and the Master's ordered me to fill it up. I've put down your ages to within a year or so, and you're to 'Return' your follerers, if any, how many, and state 'P'lice or Military,' fees and tips from Tradesmen and Wisitors 'per Ann.,' price o' kitchen-stuff, average o' breakages, &c., &c.'

## 'THE MAN THAT HATH NOT MUSIC,' &c.

*Brown (musical) invites his Highland friend, McClanky, to stay for a few days with him. But McClanky was musical too!*
*McClanky (the next morning)*. 'Will I give you a chune?'
*Brown (he had wondered what was in that green bag!)*. 'Oh - eh? Thanks, very much!' *(Puts on invalid expression.)* 'But my Doctor tells me I must on no account indulge my passion for music for some time!'

## ASSURING!

*Passenger (faintly)*. 'C'lect fares—'fore we get across! I thought we—'
*Mate*. 'Beg y'r pardon, sir, but our orders is, in bad weather, to be partic'lar careful to collect fares, 'cause in a gale like this 'ere, there's no knowing how soon we may all go to the bottom!'

## 'COMPLIMENTS OF THE SEASON.'

*Guest*. 'It's very kind of you to—'
*Hosts*. 'Oh, we should not have felt comfortable unless we'd come with you, and—seen the last of you—'!!

**THE GENTLE CRAFTSMAN (?)**
*Irascible angler (who hasn't had a rise all day).*
'There!'—*(Throwing his fly-book into the stream, with
a malediction)*—'Take your choice!'

- 32 -

**ALL THE DIFFERENCE!**
*Haberdasher (to assistant who has had the 'swop').* 'Why has that lady gone without buying?'
*Assistant.* 'We haven't got what she wants.'
*Haberdasher.* 'I'll soon let you know, Miss, that I keep you to sell what I've got,
and not what people want!'

*Ever since poor Jenkins met with that accident in the hansom cab
last fortnight, his nocturnal slumbers have been agitated by a constantly
recurring nightmare. He dreams that a more than usually appalling
cab-horse bolts with him in Hanway Passage (Oxford Street); And
cannot quite make out whether he is riding in the cab, or whether it is he
who stands, powerless to move, right in front of the infuriated animal..*

*BE-FOGGED*
*Polite old gentleman (in the fog).* 'Pray, sir,
can you kindly tell me if I'm going right for
London Bridge?' *Shadowy stranger.*
'Lum Bri'gsh? Goo' joke! 'Nother man 'shame
shtate's myshelf! I wan't' fin' Lum Bri'gsh, too!
Ta' my arm—' *[Old gent hurries off!*

George du Maurier, 1885

**EXPERIENTIA DOCET?**

*Wife of two years' standing.* 'Oh yes! I'm sure he's not so fond of me as at first. He's away so much, neglects me dreadfully, and he's so cross when he comes home. What shall I do?'
*Widow.* 'Feed the brute!'

George du Maurier, 1874

**TERRIBLE RESULT OF THE HIGHER EDUCATION OF WOMEN!**

*Miss Hypatia Jones, Spinster of Arts (on her way to refreshment), informs Professor Parallax, FRS, that 'young men do very well to look at, or to dance with, or even to marry, and all that kind of thing!' But that 'as to enjoying any rational conversation with any man under fifty, that is completely out of the question!'*

Charles Keene, 1869

**ZOOLOGY**

*Railway Porter (to old lady travelling with a menagerie of pets).* ''Station Master say, Mum, as cats is 'dogs,' and rabbits is 'dogs,' and so's parrots; but this ere 'tortis' is an insect, so there ain't no charge for it!'

- 34 -

THE "ÉDITION DE LUXE."

George du Maurier, 1883

**FOND AND FOOLISH**
*Edwin (suddenly, after a long pause).* 'Darling!'
*Angelina.* 'Yes, darling!?' *Edwin.* 'Nothing, darling. Only darling, darling!'
*[Bilious Old Gentleman feels quite sick.]*

**'IN CONFIDENCE.'**
*Dining-room, Apelles Club. Diner.* 'Thompson, do the members
ask for this wine?' *Head waiter (sotto voce).* 'Not twice, sir!'

**GOOD ADVERTISEMENT**
'I used your soap two years ago; since then I have
used no other.'

# New Technology

The dizzying pace of technological change in the nineteenth century provoked many encounters (painful and otherwise) with the new developments. The wonders of photography were appreciated by all the social classes, but John Leech's London businessmen were less convinced of the benefits of the telegraph. Labour-saving devices may have given the ladies time on their hands but were sometimes extra effort for the servants.

John Leech, 1862

**POSITIVE FACT, OF COURSE**
*A message comes off on Mrs Bluebag's linen, which she is hanging, as usual, on the telegraph wires.*

John Leech, 1863

**THE DISTRICT TELEGRAPH. INVALUABLE TO THE MAN OF BUSINESS**
*First Partner (to Second ditto).* 'What an age we live in! Talk of the introduction of steam or gas! Just look at the facilities afforded by electricity. It is now six o'clock, and we are in Fleet Street, and this message was only sent from Oxford Street yesterday afternoon at three!'

Charles Keene, 1866

**THE SEWING-MACHINE**
*Draper.* 'A most wonderful invention, indeed, mum, and it really executes the work so efficiently and quickly that, 'pon my word, I think there's nothing left for the ladies to do now but to improve their intellects!'

**MEETING A GAS-METER.**

**SUCH AN UNEXPECTED PLEASURE!**

*The great advantage of having the electric light 'brought to your very door,' without any previous notice, on the identical day, too, when you are giving a party, and your friends won't be able to get within some yards of your house. And then, so nice for ladies if it rains!*

**THE ELECTRIC AGE.**

*(Will it cause a strike?)* 'What with the guvnor's telephone and the missus's hot plate and Miss Mabel's new electric toaster, breakfast is now one long blooming hurdle-race.'— *Jeames's letter to a friend.*

**PHOTOGRAPHIC BEAUTIES**

'I say, mister, here's me and my mate wants our fotergruffs took; And mind, we wants 'em 'ansom, cos they're to give the two ladies.'

George du Maurier, 1881

**HARE AND HOUNDS—AND MAY THEIR SHADOWS NEVER GROW LESS**
*Mrs Miniver.* 'How exhausted they look, poor fellows! Fancy doing that sort of thing for mere pleasure!' *Little Timpkins (his bosom swelling with national pride).* 'Ah, but it's all through doing that sort of thing for mere pleasure, mind you, that we English are—what we are!' *[Bully for little Timpkins!]*

George du Maurier, 1891

**TELEPHONIC COMMUNICATION**
*Husband (off to Paris).* 'Don't cry, darling. It's too sad to leave you, I know! But you can talk me there just as if we were together—only be careful, as it's expensive!' *Wife.* 'Is it, darling? Ha-ha-hadn't you better leave me a few blank cheques?'

Phil May, 1894

**FOGGY WEATHER**
'Has Mr Smith been here?'
'Yes; He was here about an hour ago.'
'Was I with him?'

Harry Furniss, 1887

**HOW WE ADVERTISE NOW.**

George du Maurier, 1893

**THE OLD COUNTRY**

*St Wycliffe's College, Oxbridge. Mr Jonah P Skeggs, from
Chicago (with his family) suddenly bursts on Jones, who keeps a letter A in the
cloisters.* 'Sir—we offer you—many apologies—for this—unwarrantable intru-
sion! We were not aware the old ruin was inhabited!'

# GEORGE DU MAURIER

## 1834-1896

The exquisite satirist of the pretensions and pomposity of high society, George du Maurier was perhaps lodged in the role by *Punch*'s editor Mark Lemon – du Maurier himself wrote 'I have generally stuck to the 'classes' because C.K. [Charles Keene] seems to have monopolised the 'masses''. One of the era's most celebrated illustrators and a member of Victorian High Bohemia, in later life, his eyesight deteriorating, du Maurier began writing novels, most famously *Trilby* with its immortal character, Svengali.

George du Maurier, 1873

**'ANSWERED.'**
'O, look here, Mr Crispin! I bought these boots here only a week ago, and they're beginning to crack already!' 'Ah, Miss! Perhaps you've been walking in them! Our boots are intended for carriage people, you know!'

George du Maurier, 1880

**NATURAL RELIGION**
*Bishop (reproving delinquent page):*
'Wretched boy! Who is it that sees and hears all we do, and before whom even I am but as a crushed worm?'
*Page*: 'The Missus my Lord!'

George du Maurier, 1884

**A LAMENT**
*Dowager*. 'It's been the worst season I can remember, Sir James! All the men seem to have got married, and none of the girls!'

George du Maurier, 1881

**NINCOMPOOPIANA (A TEST)**
*The Squire.* 'I believe it's a Botticelli.'
*Prigsby.* 'Oh, no! Pardon me! It is not a Botticelli. Before
a Botticelli I am mute!' *[The Squire wishes it was.*

George du Maurier, 1880

- 41

**THE SIX-MARK TEA-POT**
*Aesthetic Bridegroom.* 'It is quite consummate, is it not?'
*Intense Bride.* 'It is, indeed! Oh, Algernon, let us live up to it!'

George du Maurier, 1895

**TRUE HUMILITY**
*Right Reverend Host.* 'I'm afraid you've got a bad egg, Mr. Jones!'
*The Curate.* 'Oh no, My Lord, I assure you! Parts of it are excellent!'

George Morrow, 1907

*Miss -----, the versatile and charming actress, in some of her favourite roles.*

- 42 -

Gunning King, 1906

Phil May, 1897

**CHANGE OF OCCUPATION.**
*Vicar's wife (sympathisingly).* 'Now that you can't get about, and are not able to read, how do you manage to occupy the time?'
*Old man.* 'Well, Mum, sometimes I sits and thinks; And then again I just sits.'

*Mrs Mashem.* 'Bull-Bull and I have been sitting for our photographs as 'Beauty and the Beast'! *Lord Loreus (a bit of a fancier).* 'Yes; He certainly is a beauty, isn't he?'

Charles Pears, 1900

Claude Allin Shepperson, 1907

- 43

*Mrs Brown.* 'Well, I must be going in a minute.'
*Mr B.* 'What for?'
*Mrs B.* 'Why, I forgot to order the fish for dinner.'

**FOR BETTER, FOR WORSE.**
*Mistress.* 'I'm sorry you want to leave, Ellis. Are you going to better yourself?'
*Maid.* 'No, M'm; I'm going to get married.'

Charles Harrison, 1899

*How Stonehenge might be popularised if the government bought it. Suggestion gratis.*

Bernard Partridge, 1899

**THE POINT OF VIEW.**

*Exasperated old gentleman (to lady in front of him).* 'Excuse me, madam, but
my seat has cost me ten shillings, and I want to see. Your hat—'
*The lady.* 'My hat has cost me ten guineas, sir, and I want it to be seen!'

- 44 -

Leonard Raven-Hill, 1900

*Carrier.* 'Try zideways, Mrs Jones, try zideways!'
*Mrs Jones.* 'Lar' bless 'ee, John, I ain't got no zideways!'

*First tramp.* 'Why don't you go in? 'E's all right. Don't you see 'im a-waggin' his tail?' *Second tramp.* 'Yus; an' don't you see 'im a-growling? I dunno which end to believe!'

SIGNAL TO STOP ELECTRIC CARS WHEN REQUIRED

HOOK TO SECURE BUNTING ON FESTIVE OCCASIONS

UNDER GROUND    KEEP TO THE RIGHT

LOST PROPERTY

STEADYING STRAP For use outside Public Houses only.

CAB OR POLICE WHISTLE

DIRECTORY

TELEPHONE    MATCH

FIRE ALARM    LETTER

RING FOR TETHERING RESTIVE HORSES

WASTE PAPER

DOGGIE

BOOT SCRAPERS

**THE IDEAL PUBLIC UTILITY LAMP-POST**

*Tommy.* 'I wonder wedder dis 'ere is a plum or a beetle?' *Bobby.* 'Taste it.'

*Imperturbable boatman.* 'Haud up yer rod, man! Ye have 'm! Ye have 'm!'

# EARLY MOTORING

Punch was there from the start to observe the destiny of the internal combustion engine on its journey from temperamental and unreliable horse replacement to world domination. Among the perils of early motoring: dusty roads, women drivers, pedestrians and supercilious car salesmen.

George Herbert Jalland, 1912

### 'WHERE IGNORANCE IS BLISS,' & C

*He (alarmed by the erratic steering).* 'Er – And have you driven much ?

*She (quite pleased with herself).* 'Oh no – this is only my second attempt. But then, you see, I have been used to a *bicycle* for years!'

Tom Browne

Thomas Browne, 1905

**THE PASSING OF THE HORSE**

Charles Harrison, 1901

*The only way to enjoy a motor-car ride through a dusty country. Adopt costumes of the above type, hermetically sealed and warranted dust-proof.*

Arthur Wallis-Mills, 1912

**OUR MOTOR EMPORIUMS**

*No, you're wrong. The one on the left is the buyer, trying to strike the right attitude of humility before the beautiful young man of the shop.*

George Loraine Stampa, 1903

*The Owner (after five breakdowns and a spill).* "Are y-you k-keen on r-riding home?"
*His friend.* "N-not very."
*The Owner.* "L-let's l-leave it a-and walk, s-shall we?"

William Bird (Jack Butler-Yates), 1912

*The Motorists' Friendly Society have, at their own expense, it is said, started a School for Pedestrians to teach them how to get out of the way.*

**PRIMUM VIVERE, DEINDE PHILOSOPHARI.**
'Is Florrie's engagement really off, then?' 'Oh, yes. Jack wanted her to give up gambling and smoking, and goodness knows what else.' *(Chorus.)* 'How absurd!!'

*Bus conductor.* 'Emmersmith! Emmersmith! Ere ye are! Emmersmith!' ' *Liza Ann.* 'Oo er yer callin' Emmersmith? Sorcy 'ound!'

*Son of the house (to caller).* ' I wanted to see you 'cos father says you made yourself.' *Caller.* ' Yes, my lad, and I'm proud hof it.' *Son of house.* ' B-but why did you do it like that?'

Frederick Henry Townsend, 1906

Frederick Henry Townsend, 1906

**FIRST NIGHT OF AN UNAPPRECIATED MELODRAMA**
*He*. 'Are we alone?'
*Voice from the gallery*. 'No, guv'nor; But you will be to-morrow night.'

**LUNCHEON HOUR CONFIDENCES**
'Such nice young man took me out to dinner last night—such a well mannered man. D'you know, when the coffee come and 'e'd poured it in 'is saucer, instead of blowing on it like a common person, 'e fanned it with 'is 'at!'

Bernard Partridge, 1899

**IN DORSETSHIRE**
*Fair cyclist*. 'Is this the way to Wareham, please?'
*Native*. 'Yes, Miss, yew seem to me to ha' got 'em on all right!'

# PHIL MAY

## 1864-1903

**M**ay got into his stride as an illustrator during three years with the *Sydney Bulletin* in Australia. On his return to Britain publishers found May's spare yet natural-looking line perfectly suited to the new photomechanical printing methods, and with his brilliant artistry and humour he soon became a household name. May's Cockney guttersnipes and inebriated revellers were not quite *Punch*'s cup of tea when he began contributing in 1893 but brought a welcome freshness to its pages during a period of dull respectability.

Phil May, 1900

**HARD LINES!**
'Just my luck! This sort of thing always happens just when I'm invited to a party!'

Phil May, 1900

**MAFEKING NIGHT**
*(Or rather 3 am the following morning.) Voice (from above).* 'Good gracious, William! Why don't you come to bed?' *William (huskily).* 'My dear Maria, you know it's been the rule of my life to go to bed shober—and I can't posh'bly come to bed yet!'

Phil May, 1902

**A BIG ORDER**
*Stout party (to waitress).* 'Put me on a pancake, please!'

Phil May, 1897

Phil May, 1898

- 51

*Lunatic (suddenly popping his head over wall).* 'What
are you doing there?' *Brown*. 'Fishing.' *Lunatic*.
'Caught anything?' *Brown*. 'No.'
*Lunatic*. 'How long have you been there?'
*Brown*. 'Six hours.' *Lunatic*. 'Come inside!'

*Jinks*. 'I want to buy a dog. I don't know what they call the
breed, but it is something the shape of a greyhound, with a
short, curly tail and rough hair. Do you keep dogs like that?'
*Fancier*. 'No. I drowns 'em!'

Phil May, 1902

**'ARRY AND 'ARRIET'S 'OLIDAY TRIP**

*It is discouraging to reflect that the older methods of aerial navigation, such as the broom,*

*the seven league boots,*

*and the magic carpet,*

*were much simpler and more effective than the modern aeroplane.*

George Morrow, 1909

Fred Pegram, 1909

**AN UNDERGROUND IMPROMPTU**
*The Tube Step.*

Claude Allin Shepperson, 1910

*Lady (to Committee-room Clerk, who hands her a small bill announcing a forthcoming political meeting).* 'But is it possible for ladies to go to these meetings?' *Clerk.* 'Why not?' *Lady.* 'I thought they were more or less of a rough nature.' *Clerk.* 'Well, madam, we've taken every possible precaution to keep out the Suffragettes.'

# TRAGEDIES OF A SIMPLE LIFE.

THE HARD-WON BATH.

Ernest Howard Shepard, 1910

Henry R Millar, 1911

**OUT OF THEIR RECKONING.**
*Pilot.* 'Where are we?'
*Mechanician (who is taking fog soundings).*
'Piccadilly, I reckon!'

Ernest Howard Shepard, 1913

'Please, teacher, mother says can Albert David sit by 'isself this
mornin', 'cos 'e's got a touch o' the measles?'

Gunning King, 1910

*Constable (to motorist who has exceeded the speed limit).* 'And I have my doubts
about this being your first offence. Your face seems familiar to me.'

IF YOU CAN'T PUTT IN THE ORDINARY WAY,

TRY LOOKING CLOSELY AT THE BALL,

OR LOOKING CLOSELY AT THE HOLE,

OR NOT LOOKING AT EITHER.

AGAIN, SOME DO IT THIS WAY

OR THUS.

YOU MIGHT TRY ONE HAND,

OR—NO HANDS.

THEN WHY NOT THIS?

OR (BEING ON A HOLIDAY) THIS?

THIS, AGAIN, IS EXCELLENT IN DRY WEATHER.

WE DON'T RECOMMEND THIS, BUT YOU MIGHT TRY IT!

## HOLIDAY PUTTS.

MR. PUNCH'S ADVICE TO THOSE WHO FIND THEMSELVES "OFF" THIS BRANCH OF THE GAME.

Frank Reynolds, 1913

Arthur Wallis Mills, 1910

**THE SUFFRAGETTE THAT KNEW JIU-JITSU**
*The Arrest.*

Arthur Wallis Mills, 1911

*The rector.* 'Now, Molly, would you rather be beautiful or good?'
*Molly.* 'I'd rather be beautiful and repent.'

Albert Talbot Smith, 1913

*Newly-appointed territorial Colonel.* 'Look here, Sergeant-Major, I'm afraid my dog has killed your cat. I—' *Sergeant-Major (ingratiatingly).* 'Oh, it'll do it a power of good, sir.'

# THE TANGO IN THE BALL-ROOM.

As letters in the papers from amateur social reformers would have us imagine it.

And as we have actually seen it.

Lewis Baumer, 1913

# 1914-1918
## THE GREAT WAR

George Loraine Stampa, 1914

'Hello, Maria! Stopped sewing for to-day?' 'Yes, Sampson. I think there is more need of men than of pyjamas. I have decided to part with you, and shall give you to Lord Kitchener—myself! Get your hat on.'

Gunning King, 1914

*Cyclist.* 'Many recruits gone from this village?' *Shopkeeper.* 'No, sir.' *Cyclist.* 'Oh, why's that?' *Shopkeeper.* 'Well, sir, after going carefully into the matter, we, in this neighbourhood, decided to remain absolutely neutral.'

THE  HISTORY  OF  A  PAIR  OF  MITTENS.

Ernest Howard Shepard, 1914

Claude Allin Shepperson, 1915

*Small boy*. 'What's on the poster, mother?'
*Mother*. 'Only 'more gains and losses,' but whether on our side or the other it doesn't say.'

Arthur Wallis Mills, 1915

**SWEDISH DRILL.**
*First weary 'special' to second ditto*. 'I say, what's the good of all this?
We're not at war with Sweden, are we?'

William Bird, (Jack Butler Yeats), 1915

*Mr Johnkins (who has overslept himself)*. 'Ha,
the Zeppelins at last! Well, I'm glad I insisted on
everyone sleeping in the basement.'

David Wilson, 1915

**FIRST CAUSES**

*Scene.—A very primitive seaside place.*
*Ancient and philosophic mariner.* 'Ay, ay. This war has come on us for our vanity.
And there never was as much vanity in Babylon as there was in Port Mugglesby last summer.'

Frank Reynolds, 1915

**THE ALIEN QUESTION.**

*Sympathetic stranger (after lady's repeated calls of 'John! John! John!').* 'John doesn't seem to be a very
obedient little dog.' *Lady.* 'Well, you see, his name isn't John; *(faintly)* It's really Fritz.'

**THE SLACKER.**

*Registrar of women workers.* 'What can I do for you?'
*Applicant.* 'You probably want a forewoman:
Somebody who is used to giving orders and words for command.
I've brought my husband to speak for me.'

*Recruiting officer.* 'I 'm afraid you won't get past the doctor.'
*Puny but pugnacious recruit.* 'I bet it won't be for the want o'
tryin'. Where is 'e?'

**FROM THE RECRUIT'S POINT OF VIEW.**
*Sergeant.* 'Form fours!' 'As you were! Form fours!!' 'As you were!!
Form fours!!!' '***!!! ****!!!!'

*George Loraine Stampa, 1915*

*Young wife (at sound of explosion).* 'Thomas! Thomas! The zeppelins are here!
Did you lock the front door?'

*Lewis Baumer, 1915*

'Well, madam, we sell a good many of both. The solid rubber is perhaps the more
serviceable article, but the other is generally considered the more becoming.'

*Bored sentry.* 'Come along! 'Urry up and take a turn at watchin' this bloomin' turnip.'

**THE USES OF A ZEPPELIN.**
*Social barriers broken down.*

How Sir Benjamin Goldmore and his junior clerk used to pass one another if they met in the City——

——And how they pass one another now.

Lewis Baumer, 1915

*Fickle young thing (revisiting tattooist.)* 'Er—do you think you could possibly alter this badge on my arm? You see, I've—er— exchanged into another regiment.'

*Boy scout.* 'Sketching the harbour's not allowed.'
*Artist.* 'Confound you! My name's Cadmium Brown, and—'
*Boy scout.* 'Carry on, then. We've got orders to treat you as harmless.'

*Vague Tommy (writing letter).* 'Wot day is it?' *Chorus.* 'The fourteenth.'
*Tommy.* 'Wot month?' *Chorus.* 'October.' *Tommy.* 'Wot year?'

*Sergeant-Major.* 'Fall out anyone that knows anything about motor-cars.'
*(Cadet falls out.)* 'Now then, what do you know about 'em?'
*Cadet.* 'Well, sir, I own a Rolls-Royce.'
*Sergeant-Major.* 'Oh, do you? Well, go and clean the adjutant's motor-cycle.'

Claude Allin Shepperson, 1916

*Our Amazon Corps 'Standing Easy.'*

R H Brock, 1916

'How is it you're not at the Front, young man?' 'Cause there ain't no milk at that end, mum.'

John Wingat, 1916

*Tommy.* 'Hello, Fritz! Bound for England like myself?'
*Fritz.* 'Ja wohl! Bot not mit a retorn teecket—tank gootness!'

George Loraine Stampa, 1916

*Doctor.* 'Do you know anything about hypodermic injection?'
*VAD nurse (late of Frivolity Theatre).* 'Rather! That's how I used
to poison a cabinet minister every night in Lady Chaterley's flat.'

Frederick Henry Townsend, 1916

*Uncle James (out with his niece).* 'Two to St Paul's, please.
Take for a lady inside—dressed in blue.'
*Bus conductress.* 'Do you mean the lady with a panné
French sailor, tête de nègre Georgette blouse, organdi collar
and an all-in-one navy gab with dyed rat revers?'

# THE BOY WHO BREATHED ON THE GLASS IN THE BRITISH MUSEUM.

### AN ANTE-BELLUM TRAGEDY.

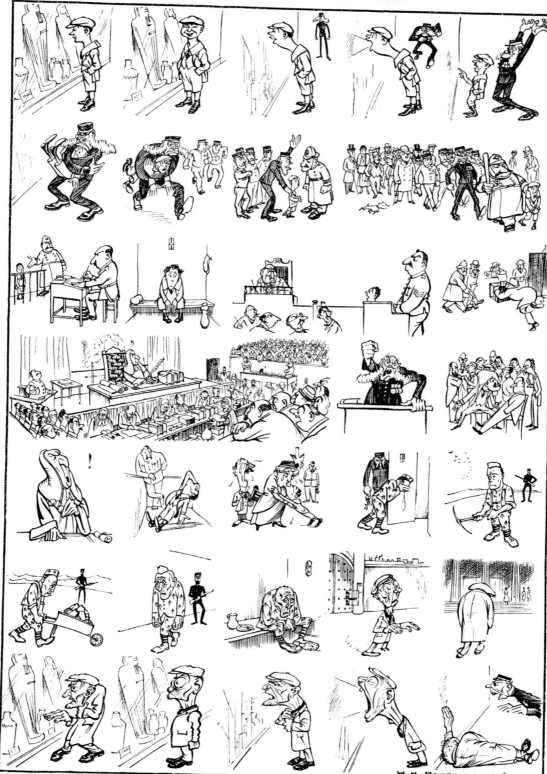

Henry Mayo Bateman, 1916

Fougasse (Kenneth Bird), 1918

"GADGETS."

George Loraine Stampa, 1917

'Wonder 'ow the navy's gettin' on.'
'Dunno. Ain't seen 'em about lately.'

Fred Pegram, 1916

*Visitor (at private hospital).* 'Can I see Lieutenant
Barker, please?' *Matron.* 'We do not allow
ordinary visiting. May I ask if you're a relative?'
*Visitor (boldly).* 'Oh, yes! I'm his sister.'
*Matron.* 'Dear me! I'm very glad to meet you,
I'm his mother.'

Lewis Baumer, 1917

'Well, upon my word! After all the trouble I had to get a quarter of a pound
of butter, the cook's sent up margarine. I should hate the maids to go short,
but I do think we ought to share things.'

Claude Allin Shepperson, 1917

*Major-general (addressing the men before practising an attack behind the lines).*
I want you to understand that there is a difference between a rehearsal and the real
thing. There are three essential differences: First, the absence of the enemy.
Now *(turning to the regimental sergeant-major)* what is the second difference?'
*Sergeant-major*. 'The absence of the general, sir.'

Arthur Wallis Mills, 1917

*Officer*. 'I say—look here. I told you to go to Paddington,
and you're going in the opposite direction.'
*Taxi-driver*. 'Orl right—orl right! You're lucky to get a cab at all,
instead of grumblin' abaht where yer wants ter go to!'

James Henry Dowd, 1917

*Awe-struck Tommy (from the trenches)*. 'Look, Bill—soldiers!'

George Loraine Stampa, 1917

**THE AMATEUR DETECTIVE.**

Frederick Henry Townsend, 1917

*Stage manager*. 'The elephant's putting up a very spirited performance to-night.'
*Carpenter*. 'Yessir. You see, the new hind-legs is a discharged soldier,
and the front legs is an out-and-out pacifist.'

George Morrow, 1917

*Sympathetic passer-by*. 'What's the matter with your little brother?'
*The sister*. 'Please, Miss, 'e's worryin' about Russia.'

Frank Reynolds, 1918

**'WAR PICTURES.'**
*The mother*. 'Of course I don't understand them, dear;
But they give me a dreadful feeling. I can't bear to look at
them. Is it really like that at the front?'
*The warrior (who has seen terrible things in battle)*.
'Thank heaven, no, mother.'

Lewis Baumer, 1918

*Alarming aunt.* 'Well, have you found any war-work yet?'
*Niece.* 'N—not exactly. B—but I've made a start.'
*Alarming aunt.* 'What have you done?'
*Niece.* 'Well, I—I've c—cut my hair off.'

Arthur Ferrier, 1918

*First Officer (in spasm of jealousy).* 'Who's the knock-kneed chap with your sister, old man?'
*Second Officer.* 'My other sister.'

THE ART OF EXTRACTION.

Lewis Baumer, 1916

*First Contemptible.* 'D'you remember, halting here on the retreat, George?'
*Second Ditto.* 'Can't call it to mind, somehow. Was it that little village in the wood there down by the river, or was it that place with the cathedral and all them factories?'

*First pessimist.* 'I'm glad it's over; It's been a terrible time.
But think what the next war will be like!'
*Second pessimist.* 'Yes—and the next peace!'

# 1919-1938

## BETWEEN THE WARS

Lewis Baumer, 1919

'Is that an official letter you are writing, Miss Brown?'
'It's—semi-official, sir.' 'What do you mean by
semi-official?' 'Well, sir—it's to an officer.'

Peter Fraser, 1919

'Where you bin this hour of the night?'
'I've bin at me union, considerin' this 'ere strike.'
'Well—you can stay down there an' consider this 'ere lock-out.'

James Henry Dowd, 1919

Standing lady. 'My husband was made a colonel just before the Armistice.'
Seated ditto. 'My husband would have been a general if it hadn't been for the war.'

The general (showing his nieces round club).
*'There's been a lot of arm-chair fighting done in this room.'*
School-girl. *'How topping! That beats pillow-fighting.*
*But isn't it rather dangerous?'*

**POST-WAR PROBLEMS**
Adjutant (who has been interrupted in his
real work by a summons from colonel). *'Yes, sir?'*
Temporary colonel. *'I say—er—Smith—it's so uncertain how long we*
*shall be out here—demobilisation, you know. Er—fact is—do*
*you think it worth my while getting another pair of breeches?'*

Peter (languidly, to hostess). *'Thank you for the party.*
*I haven't enjoyed myself much, but it doesn't matter.'*

THE MAN WHO GOT HIS MONEY'S WORTH.

George Loraine Stampa, 1919

Frank Reynolds, 1919

Mother. '*George were always a turrible one to clean 'isself;
But the army do seem to 'ave made un worse.*'
Father. '*Ah! 'E gives way to it.*'

A Thompson, 1919

**SCENE—COLOGNE—PRESENT DAY.**
'*Gie ye chocolate! Gie ye chocolate!! D'ye think I've
been bobbin' up an' doon in front o' your auld mon for
four years just tae come here an' gie ye chocolate?*'

Lewis Baumer, 1921

'*That's Betty Grant's new maid.*' '*She's much smarter than her mistress.*'
'*Well, they can't both afford to dress like that.*'

Frank Reynolds, 1919

Shortsighted traveller. *'Is there some delay on the line, my good man?'*
Naval officer. *'Who the — do you think I am, sir?'*
Traveller. *'Er—n-not the vicar, anyway.'*

Ricardo Brook, 1919

**THE THIRST FOR EDUCATION**
Mother. *'Wot's all this 'ubbub goin' on indoors?'*
Daughter. *'Baby's bin and licked 'Erbert's 'ome
lessons orf 'is slate.'*

Lewis Baumer, 1920

Old-fashioned aunt. *'Good heavens, child! You're not going out like that?
You look like a chorus-girl.'* Modern maiden. *'Oh, come, aunt!
I don't look as horribly respectable as that, surely?'*

# THE MAN WHO COULD DO IT HIMSELF.

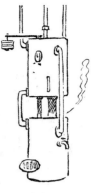

*'Horace, there's something wrong with the boiler. Shall I get the plumber?'*

*'Plumber? Of course not –*

*I'll put it right*

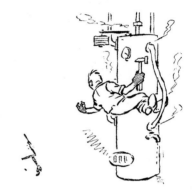

*Just get me a spanner –*

*and a hammer –*

*and a ladder –*

*and some string –*

*and a wooden plug or two –*

*and as many towels as you can find –*

*and all the blankets in the house –*

*and –*

*the doctor.'*

Fougasse (Kenneth Bird), 1920

Officer. *'When you see a moon like that, Thompson,
doesn't it sometimes make you feel a little bit sentimental?'*
P.O. *'No, sir, I can't say it do. The on'y time I gets sloppy
now is when I've 'ad a few nice-lookin' pints o' beer.'*

Pedestrian. *'Dropping anything, mister?'* Motorist. *'Yes.'*
Pedestrian. *'What is it?'* Motorist. *'My girl.'*

- 84 -

Fond and resourceful Mother. *'It's baby's birthday to-morrow. He's too young to
invite children, so I'm having fifteen people in to play bridge.'*

Lewis Baumer, 1919

Little girl (to bride at wedding reception). *'You don't look nearly as tired as I should have thought.'*
Bride. *'Don't I, dear? But why did you think I should look tired?'*
Little girl. *'Well, I heard Mummy say to Dad that you'd been running after Mr Goldmore for months and months.'*

Bertram Prance, 1920

Mr Meere. *'You'll really have to be more careful, dear,*
*how you speak to the cook or she'll be leaving us.'*
Mrs M. *'Perhaps I was rather severe.'* Mr M. *'Severe!*
*Why, anyone would have thought you were talking to me.'*

IT'S ALL IN THE GAME.

Henry Mayo Bateman, 1920

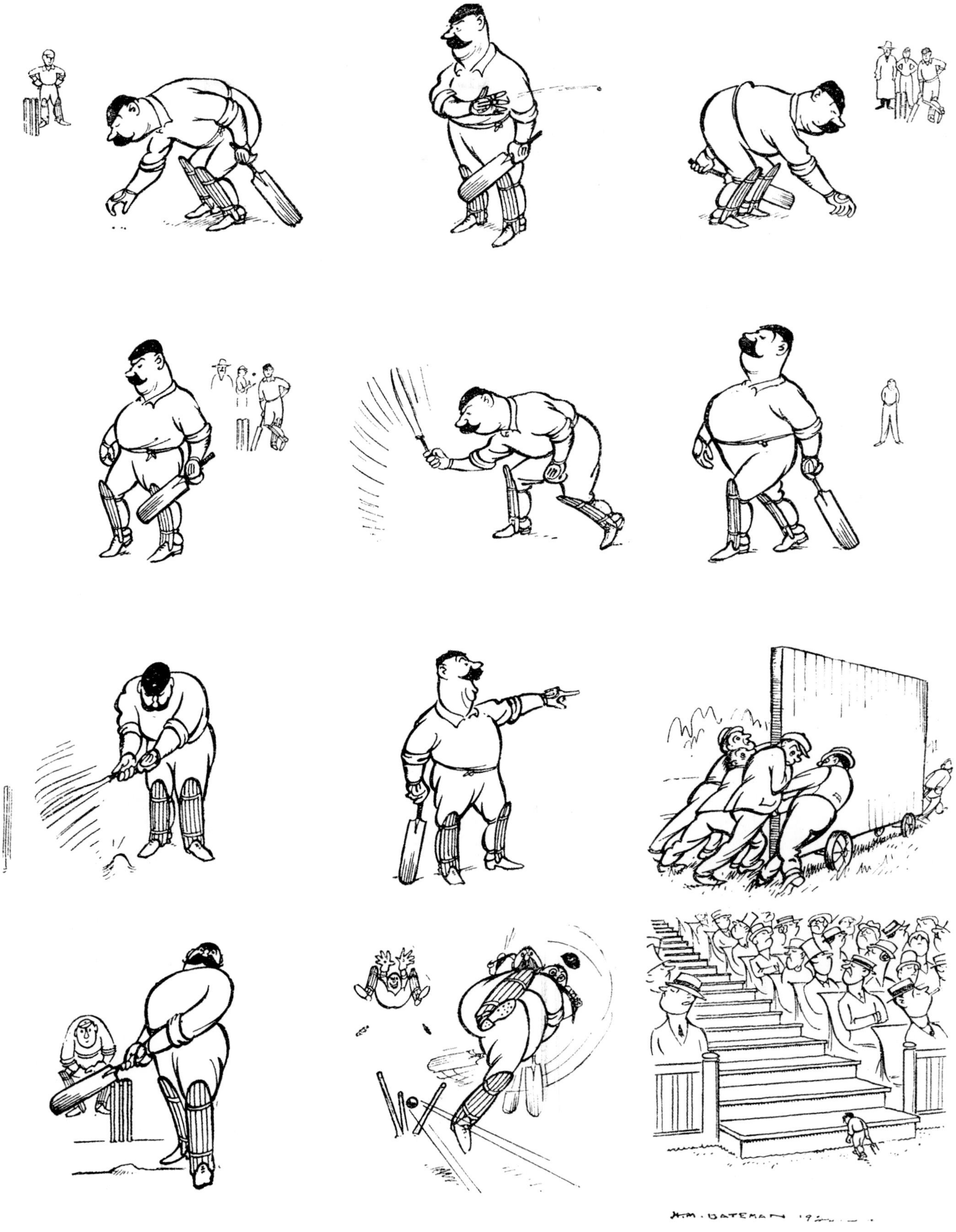
H.M. BATEMAN

Henry Mayo Bateman, 1920

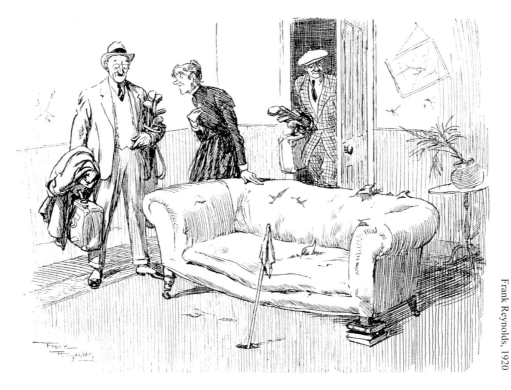

Frank Reynolds, 1920

**HOLIDAY GOLF**
Landlady (showing apartments in the vicinity of famous links).
*'Oh, you'll be quite comfortable here, sir; You see we're used to golfers.'*

- 88 -

Peter Fraser, 1921

*'Wot's a minimum wage, Albert?'*
*'Wot yer gets for goin' to yer work. If yer wants*
*ter make a bit more yer does a bit o' work for it.'*

Leonard Raven-Hill, 1920

Farmer. *'I wonder what some of these*
*London folks 'ud say to this?'*
Farm-hand. *'Zay? They'd zay as we must*
*be makin' our fortunes out o' mushrooms.'*

Lewis Baumer, 1919

**OUR DANCING MEN**

*'Who's the slightly ancient dame that that kid Binks has been dancing with all the evening?'*
*'I dunno. Young Binks doesn't either. But he says she's the only*
*woman in the room with a glimmering of how to 'jazz.''*

George Denholm Armour, 1925

He. *'That's the new man who's taken The Court, isn't it? I wonder if he's good to hounds?'*
She. *'Oh, yes—quite, I think. I saw him giving a sandwich to one the other day.'*

Fougasse, 1937

*'There's a moose loose!' 'Are you English or Scots?'*

# H M Bateman

## 1887-1970

Bateman's celebrated series *The Man Who...* first appeared in *Tatler* in 1912, but *Punch* was the lucky recipient of many of the most famous, including 'The Boy Who Breathed on the Glass in the British Museum' (*see* page 69). Australian-born Bateman was hugely successful, illustrating for many of the major magazines and advertisers of the day. Master of the multi-image cartoon story, his characters insouciantly breech social conventions to the horror of onlookers, or exude a barely suppressed rage.

Henry Mayo Bateman, 1922

**THE MAID WHO WAS BUT HUMAN**

Henry Mayo Bateman, 1922

**THE GREAT STRIKE**

Henry Mayo Bateman, 1922

**THE COCKTAIL KING**

# A FREE KICK SHALL BE AWARDED IF—

any player –

being –

on –

the ground –

does not –

immediately –

get –

up.

Fougasse (Kenneth Bird), 1921

George Belcher, 1921

Bert Thomas, 1922

Lady. *'Is it really necessary to use such dreadful expressions whilst you work?'*
Plumber. *'No, Mum, it ain't exactly necessary, but the quality of the work will suffer if we don't.'*

Golfer (after the fourth miss). *'Dear me!*
*Whatever can I be thinking about?'*
Caddie. *'Mebbe ye're thinkin' aboot yer new breeks.'*

- 93 -

Charles Grave, 1921

*'Mrs Coote, what precautions, if any, do you take against moths getting into my clothes?'*
*'Well, sir, if I sees any flying about I slashes at 'em.'*

Ernest Howard Shepard, 1922

Mother. *'Jean, darling, you mustn't be vain. Nobody will like you.'*
Jean. *'Oh, won't they? Well, I shall.'*

- 94 -

Lewis Baumer, 1923

*As she fondly hoped she appeared when executing her famous volley.*

*As the camera (which, presumably, cannot lie) told her she appeared.*

THE MISSING STAMP.

Henry Mayo Bateman, 1922

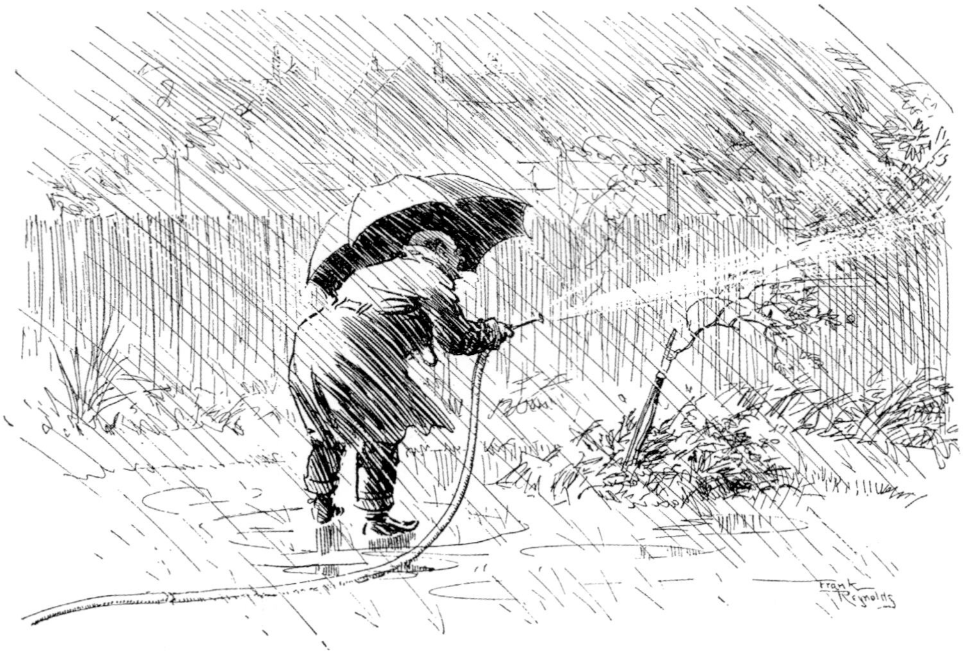
Frank Reynolds

Frank Reynolds, 1922

**FOR THIS RELIEF…**
*At last we can use the new hose with a clear conscience.*



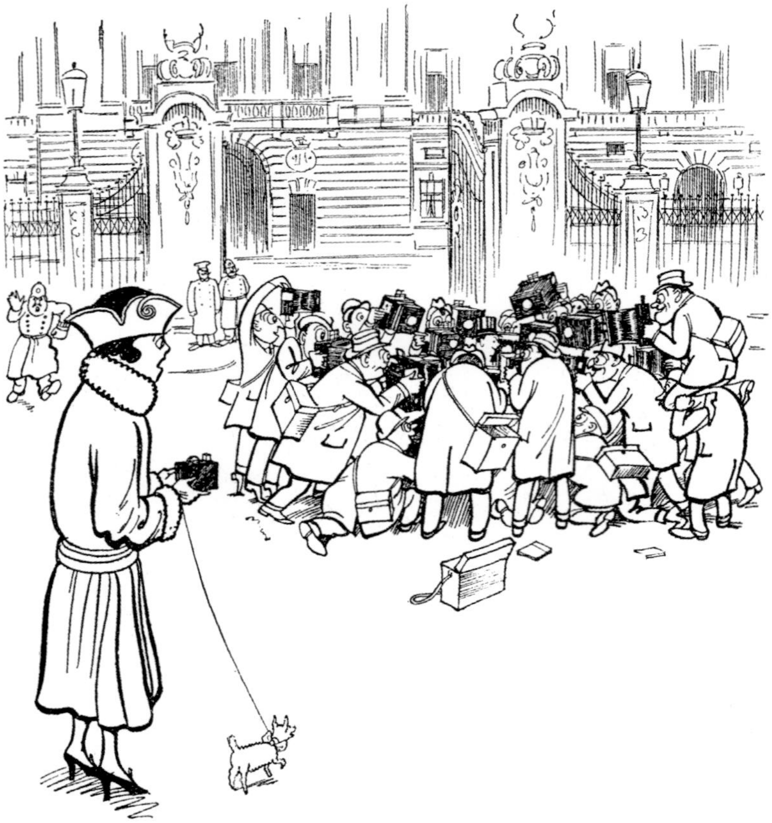

Henry Mayo Bateman, 1922

**THE GIRL WHO THOUGHT SHE WOULD LIKE A SNAPSHOT OF THE PRINCE**

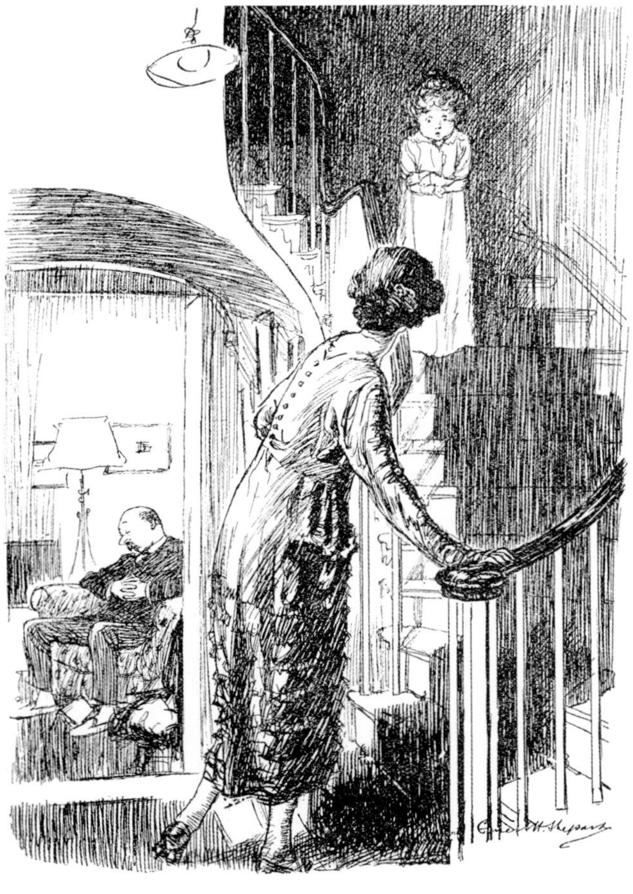

Ernest Howard Shepard, 1921

Small girl. *'Mummy, I'm frightened of bogey-man up here by myself.'*
Mother. *'You're quite safe, dear; Daddy's downstairs.'*

THE BEGUILER.

James Affleck Shepherd. 1923

- 98 -

W. Heath Robinson, 1923

## SEASIDE CRIME.

*Elaborate plot engineered by notorious gang of seaside thieves to steal a child's pail.*

Bert Thomas, 1923

Hotel proprietor. *'I'm sorry you consider the bill excessive.*
*The hotel has the reputation of being very moderate.*
Visitor. *'It certainly is—all but the charges.'*

James Henry Dowd, 1924

**OUR INFORMATIVE PRESS**

George Loraine Stampa, 1923

**Christmas Shopper.** *'Have you any sort of thing, about fourpence, to amuse a father?'*

Doctor. *'What did you operate on Jones for?'*
Surgeon. *'A hundred pounds.'*
Doctor. *'No, I mean what had he got?'*
Surgeon. *'A hundred pounds.'*

Village dame. *'The auld laird hadna seen ye for thretty-
five years, and he kenned ye? Weel, weel!'*
Sandy. *'Na, I wanna say that, but he kenned
ma coat an' breeks.'*

Percy. *'Does it always rain in this ghastly place?'*
Boatman. *'Lor' bless yer, no, sir. Why, only last summer
a London gent went 'ome with sunstroke.'*

George Morrow, 1925

**BRIGHTER LONDON**
*Speeding up the escalator.*

Henry Matthew Brock, 1924

Policeman (producing note-book). *'Name, please.'*
Motorist. *'Aloysus—Alastair—Cyprian—'*
Policeman (putting book away). *'Well, don't let me catch you again.'*

David Louis Ghilchik, 1925

**PERILS OF THE DANCE**
*The terror of the Oxford trousers.*

Frank Reynolds, 1921

Small boy (walking round with his father). *'Daddy, here's a ball for you.'* Father. *'Where did you get that from?'* Small boy. *'It's a lost ball, Daddy.'* Father. *'Are you sure it's a lost ball?'* Small boy. *'Yes, Daddy; They're still looking for it.'*

Frank Hart, 1925

Returned traveller. *'But most of the South Sea Islanders have long since given up cannibalism.'* Young hostess. *'Really! They're still quite interesting, though, aren't they?'*

Self-satisfied Tyro (who in spite of disregarding expert advice has caught a 'fish'). *'I was a bit too cunning for that one, Duncan.'* Duncan (gloomily extracting the fly). *'Ay, there's daft idjits in the watter as weel's oot o'it.'*

*'You can't marry Greta Garbo until you grow up, so do stop being a baby about it.'*

*'How much did you say? Seventeen guineas? Very moderate. Put it down to me, will you?'* *'Excuse me, sir,—but—we have rather a large account against you. It's—er—getting a little difficult—'* *'No, really! I'll send my man along; He's a remarkable fellow—he'll add it up for you in no time, good morning.'*

She. *'A dangerous woman—with a past.'* He. *'Well, let her bury it, poor creature.'*
She. *'She can't. It's not dead yet.'*

- 104 -

Lady (to new housemaid engaged by letter). *'Why didn't you tell me, when you wrote answering my questions so fully, that you were Scotch, Mary?'* Mary. *'I didna like to be boasting, mem.'*

Wife (in a panic). *'Oh, Jack, Jack! Baby's been and swallowed a sixpence!'* Husband. *Oh, well, my dear, one can't buy much for sixpence nowadays.'*

Driver (rounding a corner on two wheels). *'You didn't know I could drive a car, did you, old man?'* 'Old man' (ageing rapidly). *'N-n-no. can you?'*

*'Did you say chocolate eclair OR meringue?'*

Salesman. *'And what kind of horn would you like, sir? Do you care for a good loud blast?'* Haughty customer. *'No; I want something that just sneers.'*

Villager on left (referring to new memorial stone). *'Pretty, ain't it?'*
Other villager (an incurable pessimist). *'Ah, so tis. But you mark my words, Mr Jubbins: The first earthquake as happens along, down she comes!'*

Frank Reynolds, 1925

Lady (trying to get seats for very popular musical comedy).
*'If I come back in an hour's time do you think it would be any
good?'* Box-office official. *'No, madam.'* Lady. *'But sometimes
tickets are returned—people die.'* Box-office official. *'Nobody
would think of dying before they've seen this show.'*

Kenneth Beauchamp, 1925

**OUR EXCLUSIVES**
*'Do you never read the weeklies?' 'Never. One feels that the
only paper one could read with interest would be understood
by so few people that it could never be published.'*

Henry Matthew Brock, 1925

Lodger (to exorbitant landlady). *'I say, I wish you'd come and score for us
in our cricket-match to-morrow.'*

# ALL THINGS TO ALL RANKS.

How to dance with—

*A subaltern.*

*A captain.*

*A major*

*and a colonel.*

Lewis Baumer, 1925

Henry Matthew Brock, 1925

Frank Reynolds, 1925

Motorist (who is lost). *'Is this the road to St Ives?'* Yokel. *'Dunno.'*
Motorist. *'Is that the road to Willingham?'* Yokel. *'Dunno.'*
Motorist. *'Well, can you tell me which is the road to Cottenham?'*
Yokel. *'Dunno.'* Motorist (exasperated). *'Well, you don't seem to
know much.'* Yokel. *'Maybe not; but I ain't lost.'*

Rugby player (to fiancé at half-time). *'Phyllis,
I think you know Johnson?'* Phyllis. *'Do I?'*

Kenneth Beauchamp, 1926

She. *'That's the Trevor girl. Fancy, she's only eighteen!'* He. *'But she
doesn't look like a girl of eighteen.'* She. *'No girl of eighteen ever does.'*

Visitor (after one night's stay at a hotel). *'There's a slight mistake here. I didn't have any coffee or liqueur or cigar last night, nor early tea this morning.'* Cashier. *'No, sir, but your chauffeur did.'*

Husband (to listening-in wife). *'What's the matter, dear?*
*Is it bad news or Stravinsky?'*

George Belcher, 1925

George Loraine Stampa, 1925

Proud father (to son home for half-term holiday). *'I supppose the boys sometimes talk of their fathers. Have you told them that I'm, a lawyer?'*
Son. *'I did tell one of my pals and he was awfully decent about it.'*

*'Where's yer father? 'As 'e gone to work?' 'I see 'im goin' dahn the street, but 'e wasn't goin' to work.'*
*''Ow d'you know?' 'Well, 'e were runnin'.'*

Nicolas Bentley, 1934

*'I say, may I have my last dance with you, Miss Butler?'*
*'Well, as a matter of fact you've already had it.'*

James Henry Dowd, 1926

Fair critic. *'Mr and Mrs Jones always give one the impression
that they both realise they have married beneath them.'*

Bertram Prance, 1927

Visitor. *'Who is the responsible man in this firm?'*
Office boy. *'I don't know who is responsible, sir,
but I always get the blame.'*

George Morrow, 1926

*A SCHOOL FOR JUDGES WHO HAVE LOST TOUCH WITH EVERYDAY LIFE.*

George Loraine Stampa, 1926

Frank Reynolds, 1926

Teacher. *'When is your little brother coming
to Sunday-school, Alfred?'*
Alfred. *'Please, Miss, mother don't wish 'im
to take up religion just yet.'*

- 112 -

Hostess (to guest who has arrived in dinner-jacket).
*'Of course I think it looks perfectly sweet, dear. But
what does your husband say?'* Guest. *'Oh, that's all
right—we've each got our own.'*

W Smithson Broadhead, 1919

*'I didn't know you knew the funny man, sis.'*
*'I didn't. But by the time I discovered that I didn't—well, I did.'*

Lewis Baumer, 1928

Newly-affianced young lady (who is never going to forget the dance she has just had).
*'Can you tell me the name of that lovely tune you just played?'*
Member of orchestra. *'Certainly. It's called "I Do Like My Little Drop of Beer."'*

Kenneth Beauchamp, 1926

### OUR CRICKET WEEK
*'This man Tommy's brought down says he's a bowler.
Do you know what he's like?' 'Yes, you know the sort
of stuff. Looks as if it's simple—and it is.'*

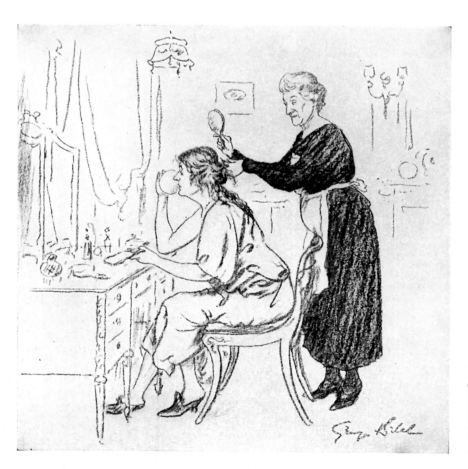

George Belcher, 1926

Mistress. *'Tell me, Grey—you've been in service a long while—what is the
cause of this difficult servant problem?'* Grey. *'Well, madam, since you ask
me, it's like this: you're going down, and we're coming up.'*

Bertram Prance, 1926

Reporter. *'To what dó you attribute your long life?'* Centenarian. *'Perseverance—just perseverance. I kep' on livin' in spite of everything.'*

Frank Reynolds, 1927

Well-meaning caddie. *'I can put you right, Miss; But, understand, you'll 'ave to sirrender yerself to me abslootly.'*

George Morrow, 1926

*DUKE WILLIAM OF NORMANDY DISCOVERS AN EXAMPLE OF SAXON MURAL DECORATION.*

Fougasse (Kenneth Bird), 1935

**NIGHTMARE.**

"NOW, YOU, SIR, IN THE FRONT ROW OF THE STALLS—LET'S HEAR YOU SING THE CHORUS BY YOURSELF."

# E H Shepard
## 1879-1976

Overshadowed by his illustrations for A A Milne's *Winnie the Pooh*, E H Shepard's association with *Punch* for over 50 years is sometimes forgotten. He contributed a huge variety of work from gag cartoons to some of the magazine's most riveting political cartoons of the interwar and war years and hundreds of superb illustrations for poems and Charivaria headings. His introduction to Milne had come through *Punch*, but Shepard tired of 'that silly old bear' and his last cartoon shows a small boy dealing a robust kick to a remarkably Pooh-like teddy.

1945

Ernest Howard Shepard, 1925

*Grannie, having been persuaded to subscribe to a charity 'lucky dip,' wins a bathing-costume and a pair of garters.*

1946

1964

Ernest Howard Shepard, 1927

Pamela. *'How's your wife, Peter?'* Peter. *'She died last Tuesday.'* Pamela. *'Are you sorry?'*
Peter. *'Sorry? Of course I'm sorry. I liked the woman.'*

Frank Reynolds, 1927

*'Will ye tak' the paper?' 'Thanks. I don't care for reading in the train.'*
*'Maybe. But will yer kindly cover yer knees wi' it? A've nae wish to contemplate them.'*

Lewis Baumer, 1927

First player. *'How ought we to divide? I'm pretty feeble.'* Second ditto. *'I expect you're a lot better than I am.'* Third ditto. *'I'm hopelessly rotten.'* Fourth ditto (ignoring the conventions). *'I'm rather hot stuff. Now let's start over again.'*

Pont (Graham Laidler), 1936

'Now, Miss Addison, if Jane is ever naughty while she's at your school.
Please just do as we do – threaten to stop her smoking during meals.'

William Bird (Jack Butler Yeats), 1931

Modern wine merchant (dictating catalogue for the
Christmas trade). *'A bizarre wine, with camaraderie,
but not of the extreme left.'*

Bert Thomas, 1928

Client. *'My wife and I got on splendidly for five years.'*
Solicitor. *'Ah! What happened then?'* Client. *'She came back.'*

Lewis Baumer, 1927

*Where men get their chance.*

Kenneth Beauchamp, 1927

PC. *'You were doing forty miles an hour, sir.'*
Motorist (whispering). *'Make it seventy; I'm trying to sell him the thing.'*

David Louis Ghilchik, 1927

'May I introduce this new little razor gadget of ours to you, sir?
It is creating a revolution in shaving.' 'No, thanks. I've tried it,
and I'm afraid it wasn't a bloodless revolution.'

Bert Thomas, 1927

The angler. 'My boy, you never saw such a fish in
your life. But, curse him! He got away from me.'
The other (hopefully). 'Did he? How?'

George Morrow, 1926

**ENTERTAINMENTS AT WHICH WE HAVE NEVER ASSISTED**
'Dropping the Pilot' at Trinity House.

George Morrow, 1927

**LESS-KNOWN SIGHTS OF THE WORLD**
*Sending off a Depression from Iceland.*

David Louis Ghilchik, 1933

**THE SLIMMING CRAZE**
Doctor. *'And do you drink at meals?'*
Patient. *'Don't be silly, doctor. Why, I don't even eat at meals.'*

James Henry Dowd, 1927

Visitor (being shown over redecorated club). *'I suppose you've replaced all these in their original positions?'*

Arthur Wallis Mills, 1927

Villager. *'I 'ear as 'ow you've bought poultry farm up at Bottom End. Do yer want to sell
any of them 'en-ouses?'* Newcomer. *'Good heavens, no! They're brand-new—only just
bought 'em.'* Villager. *'Ah, well, I bought some stuff when the two lots of folk as 'ad the farm
afore you went bust; And I can wait.'*

David Louis Ghilchik, 1927

Nervous youth. *'I—I'm sorry my shocking play lost us the set, partner.'*
Colonel O' Curry (in a vile temper). *'Aren't you going to apologise for wearing that foul hat too?'*

- 124 -

James Henry Thorpe, 1927

*'Well, Daphne, and what are you going to do when you grow up?'*
*'Oh, diet, I suppose.'*

Arthur Watts, 1928

The owner. *'But it does give you a feeling of movement?'*
The other. *'Yes, horribly.'*

Husband. *'I should have thought you'd be ashamed to show your face in such a gown.'*
Wife. *'Don't worry, darling. My face won't be the chief attraction.'*

The lady (to voluble casualty). *'One would think you had never been run over before.'*

# CHRISTMAS À L'ANGLAISE.

*They fly from England to avoid the English Christmas.*

*They arrive.*

*'Ecco, Signora! Ee English meestletoe!'*

*'Ze stocking for Signor to 'ang!'*

Ernest Howard Shepard, 1927

# CHRISTMAS À L'ANGLAISE.

*'Benissimo! Ze plom poudang.'*

*Finally, the 'Auld Land Syne' with perfect strangers is too much for them—*

*and they return to Soho for a continental meal.*

Ernest Howard Shepard, 1927

James H Thorpe, 1927

The tigress. *'Let's see—what's your handicap?'*
The rabbit. *'Twenty-four; But I'm fairly bright otherwise.'*

Fougasse (Kenneth Bird), 1938

*'It is possible to tell a man's political opinions by the newspaper he reads,'* says a magistrate. So the man who sits opposite us in the train evidently always thinks as we do.

Lewis Baumer, 1928

*'I'll tell you what, old thing, this new feminine touch is all right, but you'll have to adopt a new stance.'*

**THE YOUNG WOMAN IN BUSINESS**

The Manager. *'The head of your department complains that you come to business frivolously dressed. I don't like your tie and I don't like your socks. Alter them, please.'*

*'And, any time you happen to be passing, do drop in ... that's our little nest – the one with the window-boxes.'*

**ANOTHER RECORD**

*The Test Match that did not produce a record.*

Kenneth Beauchamp, 1929

Assistant. *'It suits Moddam perfectly.
One would think the animal died for Moddam!'*

Ernest Howard Shepard, 1929

**OUR ATHLETIC GIRLS.**
*Grannie Decides to Improve Her Figure.*

Frank Reynolds, 1928

Young husband. *'I can't stand this suspense any longer, It will kill me.'*
Doctor. *'Calm yourself, my dear sir. I've brought thousands of babies
into the world and never lost a father yet.'*

THE FIRST SCRATCH—

AND THE LAST.

Fougasse (Kenneth Bird), 1929

Lady. *'You come here begging and say you are not expected to do any more work. I never heard of such a thing.'* Tramp. *'Then I've been misinformed, lidy. I certainly 'eard that after the war England was goin' ter be a better place fer the labouring classes.'*

George Belcher, 1919

Henry Mayo Bateman, 1931

**THE MAN WHO SAID, 'FINE, THANKS!' WHEN ASKED 'HOW'S BUSINESS?'**

David Louis Ghilchik, 1931

Young man (on the subject of parlour-games). *'Personally I think Musical Chairs rather childish — don't you?'* Suburban vamp. *'Not the way I play it.'*

# HOLIDAY SNAPS.

## THE JONESES NATURALLY PUT ALL THEIR BEST HOLIDAY SNAPS IN THEIR ALBUM.

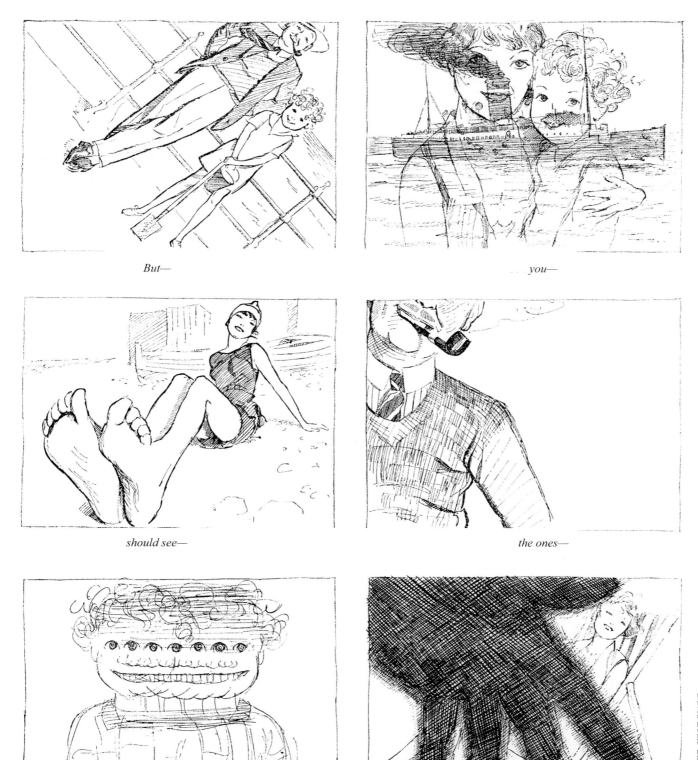

*But—*

*you—*

*should see—*

*the ones—*

*they didn't—*

*put in.*

David Louis Ghilchik, 1929

Frederick Henry Townsend, 1920

**THE JUDGMENT OF PARIS**
*The 'flapper seat' and its holiday problems.*

Arthur Wallis Mills, 1927

Lady (choosing bathing-dress). *'They're all marvellous,
but not quite deafening enough for Deauville.'*

George Morrow, 1924

Romantic lady. *'Do you ever see pictures in the fire?'*
Embittered art critic. *'No. But I've seen lots that ought to be.'*

Rick Elmes, 1930

Owner of ancient bus. *'I say, what would you advise? My car won't go on modern
brands of petrol.'* Garage-man. *'You might try some cat's meat, Guv'nor.'*

Girl (to young man who has asked for a second cherry in his cocktail). *'What's the great idea, Tony?'*
Tony. *'Family medical adviser insists I must eat more fruit.'*

Female (to friend). *'Although I live in Balham, I feel
that spiritually I belong to West Kensington.'*

**THE WOBBLE**

# THE LACQUERED LADY.

With shouts of joy Miranda hails
The craze for lacquered finger-nails;

And when the vogue still further goes
She lacquers—and displays—her toes.

Like wild-fire now the fashion spreads
From painted feet to painted heads;

Behold her, with a reckless air,
Applying lacquer to her hair.

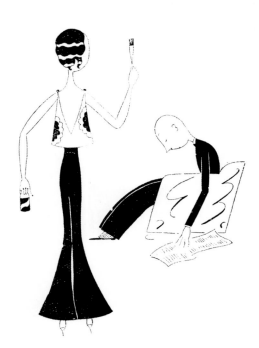

A happy thought! while Edward sleeps
Behind his chair she softly creeps . . .

And later greets his waking eyes
With "Edward, look! a nice surprise!"

Anne Harriet Fish, 1932

**THE FLIRT**

**THE NEW MOVEMENT**
Hostess. *'Will you take this chair, Uncle?'*
Uncle. *'As long as I don't have to sit on it, my dear.'*

Gloomy diner. *'Which of your beastly wines
will induce oblivion?'*

Henry Mayo Bateman, 1930

**THE MAN WHO PAID OFF HIS OVERDRAFT**

William Leigh Ridgewell, 1930

'By jove, Gladys, every time I look at that pear-tree it
makes my mouth water.'

# THE SPELL OF THE GAME.

*Fougasse*

2.30 P.M. MIDANDLEGSHIRE INNINGS OPENS.

2.45 P.M. MIDANDLEGSHIRE 3 FOR 0.

3 P.M. MIDANDLEGSHIRE 7 FOR 0.

3.15 P.M. MIDANDLEGSHIRE 11 FOR 0.

3.30 P.M. MIDANDLEGSHIRE 18 FOR 0.

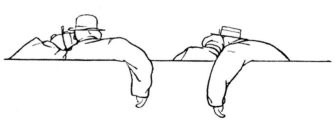

3 45 P.M. MIDANDLEGSHIRE 25 FOR 0.

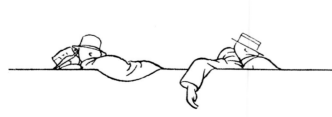

4 P.M. MIDANDLEGSHIRE 27 FOR 0.

4.15 P.M. TEA INTERVAL.

Fougasse (Kenneth Bird), 1928

William Augustus Sillince, 1938

'How has Great Britain fared in the Test Match, MacGregor?'

Bert Thomas, 1927

The wife. 'You are getting much too high-spirited, Benjamin.
I'm afraid cook makes your barley-water too strong.'

# THE BIG CUTS

It was the 'Big Cuts' – the full-page political cartoons – that gave *Punch* its power and influence. Eagerly scanned in the Houses of Parliament, the Big Cuts had the ability to wound not just the home-grown political beast. *Punch* had been banned in France, while in Germany Kaiser Wilhelm II allegedly cancelled his subscription in a huff at one of its cartoons (though he soon renewed it). In Russia the censor attacked the magazine with black paint and scissors – a scene Sambourne memorably depicted in 1878 (*see* page 10). Such were the authority of *Punch*'s Big Cuts that the two titans of the genre, John Tenniel and Bernard Partridge, were given knighthoods.

*Substance and Shadow*, Leech's *Cartoon No. 1* of 1843 (*see* page 8), first applied the term 'cartoon' to a satirical drawing and the name stuck. The cartoon mocked the government's costly exhibition of preliminary sketches (technically called 'cartoons') in a public competition for wall paintings to decorate the new Houses of Parliament. Leech's drawing was *Punch*'s 'entry' to the competition and showed a group of ragged Londoners wandering round the exhibition – there was any amount of funds available for such useless frivolities, but none apparently to better the lot of these poverty-stricken citizens of the capital.

Until well into the twentieth century choosing the subject for the Big Cut was a group effort as the editor, proprietor and staff dined round the famous *Punch* Table and discussed the burning issues of the day. Perhaps most celebrated (certainly the most parodied) of all

the Big Cuts is Tenniel's *Dropping the Pilot*, where a young Wilhelm II sends off the aged Bismarck. Here are a few of the other cartoons that achieved immortality, among them Tenniel's *The British Lion's Vengeance On The Bengal Tiger* on the aftermath of the Indian Mutiny of 1857, and his unforgettable image of Disraeli offering the crown of India to Queen Victoria in *New Crowns for Old Ones!*.

Bernard Partridge assumed Tenniel's mantle and in cartoons like *The Coming Perilette* showed he was as inventively imaginative as the old master. Partridge's *Unconquerable*, showing the Belgian King standing up to the Kaiser, was endlessly reproduced during WWI. Though not among the most celebrated Big Cut artists, Leonard Raven-Hill's *The Gap in the Bridge* on America's refusal to join the League of Nations was recently nominated one of the ten greatest political cartoons of all time.

Winston Churchill was one of the most caricatured politicians in *Punch* and images like E H Shepard's triumphal *The Dragon Slayer* added to the Churchill myth. Thirteen years later, a notorious cartoon by Leslie Illingworth showed an aged and infirm Prime Minister; Churchill was devastated and wrote '*Punch* goes everywhere. I shall have to retire if this sort of thing goes on…' This was perhaps the last time the Big Cuts had the power to inflict damage. In the 1970s *Punch* dropped its full-page political cartoons – an indication of the magazine's dwindling political clout. Though they were revived some years later, never again would the Big Cuts dominate the pages of *Punch*.

John Tenniel, 1876

**"NEW CROWNS FOR OLD ONES!"**

Bernard Partridge, 1907

**THE COMING PERILETTE**

**THE GAP IN THE BRIDGE**

**THE BRITISH LION'S VENGEANCE ON THE BENGAL TIGER**

**DROPPING THE PILOT**

- 143 -

**UNCONQUERABLE**

*The Kaiser.* 'So you see—you've lost everything.'
*The King of the Belgians.* 'Not my soul.'

**THE DRAGON-SLAYER**
*'So much for that one, and now to face the next.'*

*Man goeth forth unto his work and to his
labour until the evening.*

**LES MATELOTS**

Distracted mother (breathlessly). *'Three-and-a-'alf wit's-end
return tickets for Clacton, please.'*

Owner of Alsatian. *'Throw your arms round her—stop her!
I've lost her for a week and she's running wild.'*

Bohemian niece. *'Well, Uncle, what do you think of our set?'*
Uncle. *'They strike me as being not so much a set, my dear, as a collection of odd pieces.'*

Oldest inhabitant (to District Visitor). *'I be ninety-four and I 'aven't got an enemy in the world.'* District Visitor. *'That is a beautiful thought.'* Oldest inhabitant. *'Yes, Miss. Thank God they be all of 'em dead long ago!'*

First player. *'My wife threatens to leave me if I don't chuck golf.'* Second player. *'That sounds serious.'*
First player. *'It is serious. I shall miss her.'*

Pont (Graham Laidler), 1935

'*Of course we go flat out for the ego here.*'

Arthur Wallis Mills, 1932

Lady. '*I do hope you'll get the bath done soon. It's really most inconvenient.*'
Plumber. '*We'll do our best, lady. When's yer bath-night?*'

W Heath Robinson, 1936

**FLAT-LIFE**
*The Kitchenette.*

SUSCEPTIBLE SPECIAL CONSTABLE ON EXTRA POINT DUTY
MEETS A FRIEND.

William Leigh Ridgewell, 1932

Douglas Lionel Mays, 1936

*'D' you mind, switching off, sir? She's gainin' on me.'*

- **148** -

Arthur Wallis Mills, 1936

Owner. *'Do tell me you* loathe *it.'*

Fitz, 1932

**TAKING OUR PLEASURES SADLY.**

THE FIRST DAY ON HOLIDAY.

Frank Reynolds, 1931

'Where are you off to?' 'To the doctor. I don't like the look of my wife.'
'I'll come with you. I hate the sight of mine.'

Paul Crum (Roger Pettiward), 1937

'Would it interest you to see my son's report?' 'No.'

Arthur Wallis Mills, 1925

House-agent (to customer who is inquiring for a very modest flat).
'Ah, well, madam, that would hardly come under our
designation of a flat. What you require is more of a dwelling.'

Charles Grave, 1932

The vicar. *'You suspect hashish? But, good heavens, man, look at my collar!' Zealous customs. 'Yess, yess—plenty time. I search you under the collar in a minute.'*

Fougasse (Kenneth Bird), 1932

*'Of course, there's one thing that no foreigner will ever understand, and that's our enthusiasm for cricket.'*

Fred Pegram, 1933

*'They had the cheek to say there wasn't a single room in the whole blasted place. We were simply furious, so we told 'em who we were.' 'Really, and who were you?'*

Henry Mayo Bateman, 1932

**COUNSEL CALLS THE JUDGE 'MISTER'**

Fougasse (Kenneth Bird), 1936

'No—I—most—certainly—will—NOT—
guess—who—this—is!!!'

George Morrow, 1933

Man-eating tiger (to his child). *'Don't touch it, Willie. It's not the edible variety.'*

Serious politician. *'Utopia will never be achieved by a single party.'*
Gay young thing. *'Oh, no—there would have to be a party every night.'*

**AFTER THE GALE**
*'And what about this 'ere 'arf timberin? Shall I peel orf what's
stuck on, or shall I tack up what's blowed orf?'*

*'D'you serve lobsters?'*
*'Yessir, we serve anybody.'*

William Leigh Ridgewell, 1933

- **154** -

'We have called really, vicar, to ask your advice.
My sister and I think of trying cremation.'

Ernest Howard Shepard, 1933

'Mummy, is an actress just a disappointed film-star?'

Arthur Wallis Mills, 1933

'Look at his disgraceful tennis-shirt! Fellah's a dashed nudist.'

Arthur Watts, 1933

"DIDN'T I TELL YER NOT TO LET THE PORE OLD FELLER SEE IT, GEORGE?"

George Sherriff Sherwood, 1933

*'May I have a chair in here now, mother?' 'Just a little more patience, darling.*
*Boo-Boo hasn't quite decided where he would like to sit.'*

Pont (Graham Laidler), 1938

**THE BRITISH CHARACTER**
*A tendency to leave the washing-up till later*

George L Tement, 1933

'How long do you boil eggs, Simpson?'
'While I smoke a cigarette, ma'am, but some burn
slower than others.'

James Henry Thorpe, 1933

'If I tried to tell you anything about the subject I should
only display my abysmal ignorance. I prefer to leave
this to the lecturer.'

George Morrow, 1933

**LONDON LIFE**
*The Dickensian Society refuses the gift of a statuette of Little Nell by a modern sculptor.*

Henry Mathew Brock, 1933

Cook. *'Well, I declare, he must have been shut in the larder all the afternoon!'*
Mistress. *'Fancy him keeping quiet all that time. How patient he is!'*

George Loraine Stampa, 1925

The wife. *'I can't think where I put that bill from the dressmakers.'* The husband (in
extraordinary good spirits). *'I haven't seen it.'* The wife. *'No, I can see you haven't.'*

Arthur Watts, 1932

"RUINED, ALBERT? AND SHALL WE HAVE TO LEAVE OUR LITTLE NEST?"

# PONT
## GRAHAM LAIDLER

Graham Laidler had drawn just over a dozen cartoons for *Punch* when he began the series that was to be the source of his enduring fame – *The British Character*. The magazine soon realized what a jewel they had and when Graham Greene's new magazine *Night and Day* tried to poach Laidler in 1937 immediately put the illustrator on an unheard-of exclusive contract. His pen name came from the contraction of a family nickname, 'Pontifex Maximus'. Pont's sudden death from polio in November 1940 at the age of only thirty-two was the tragic loss of a major talent.

Pont, 1937

**THE BRITISH CHARACTER**
*A disinclination to sparkle*

Pont (Graham Laidler), 1936

**THE BRITISH CHARACTER**
*Refusal to admit defeat.*

Pont (Graham Laidler), 1933

'Thank you, Wilson, only one pair of bedsocks. I musn't be pampered.'

Pont, 1937

'Of course we must face facts. It's going to
mean waiting.'

Bert Thomas, 1933

Tramp (retiring for the night, re newspapers from which numerous coupons have been removed).
*'These blinking competitions will be the death of us.'*

- 162 -

Charles Grave, 1933

Frank Hart, 1933

*'This a ruddy fine game 'olystonin' the decks at one
o'clock in the mornin'.' 'You ain't got the right way
of lookin' at it. I gets a lot of 'appiness by bangin'
about an' keepin' passengers awake what's paid a
'undred quid for the outin'.'*

*'You seem so grown-up, Armstrong—sort of manly.
Does it take long to get like that?' 'Oh! A term or two,
but of course you have to have it in you.'*

'Now, don't tell me! I want to guess. Haven't—you—two—young
people—been sun-bathing—somewhere?'

Pont (Graham Laidler), 1934

'This is little Chromium, Auntie; but don't disturb him, he's
having his hour's recreation.'

'Did I really understand you, Miss Wilson, to use the expression,
'A cosy nook', in connection with the house you wish me to design for you?'

'Hey, Sam, I've given 'ee guard three times.'
'I knows, George, but I stands this way to fast 'uns.'

**THE MODERN HOME**
'But, my dear, why the table?'

Prudent swain (choosing Valentine). *'Perhaps you can help me, Miss; What I'm reely looking for is something frightfully ardent yet definitely non-committal.'*

*'How is the snow your way, dear? Ought I to put on chains?' 'Don't bother, darling. Wear anything you feel comfortable in.'*

*'What's it say, darling?' 'Eat more fruit.'*

*Brr—*

*'Hullo....oh, is that you, darling?... How lovely to hear your voice, my sweet..*

*What? ... Oh, my dear, how marvellous!... That's quite the most wonderful news I've had for years...*

*Darling, I'm thrilled...yes...yes...what? ...what? ... Nonsense! ... It can't be true!!!...*

*But how simply too terrible for words!!!... ...no...yes... yes...no...my dear, I can't believe it!!!...*

*Yes, awful...no, ghastly...yes, horrible no, it's just too perfectly frightful!!!... Good-night, my sweet...good-night...*

*It was only that tiresome Brown-Robinson girl—*

*No news as usual—just wanted a bit of a chat.'*

Fougasse (Kenneth Bird), 1937

Arthur Reginald Cane, 1934

'Does he get you over the jumps all right, sir?'
'Yes, he gets me over all right. The trouble is he doesn't
come with me.'

George Belcher, 1932

'I ordered whitebait, and I find shrimps and a dogfish among them.'
'Yes, it's wonderful, sir, how gregarious these little fishes are.'

Arthur Wallis Mills, 1934

'The darling! It seems only yesterday that I pulled
out the first grey hair from his dear head.'

William Leigh Ridgewell, 1934

**NUMBER FIVE RECOGNISES A FRIEND**

George Morrow, 1925

*Young Richard Whittington has a prophetic nightmare
of the way posterity will picture him.*

Pont (Graham Laidler), 1934

*'I trust, Mickelton Minimus, that you will not have the impertinence to contradict
me when I say that I perceive an element of defiance in your present bearing.'*

Fougasse, 1936

*'I think there's some mistake—
this is her mother speaking.'*

David Louis Ghilchik, 1934

*'Perkins, you must give Fi-Fi more than ordinary care.
While I'm away you must live only for her.'*

Frank Reynolds, 1926

Earnest student of the films (to superior couple who are inclined to scoff).
*'If you ain't eddicated enough to enjoy a good picture, let them as is does.'*

- **170** -

Arthur Wallis Mills, 1933

*'Darlings, I'm engaged. This damfool wants to marry me.'*

Fougasse 1937

Margaret (not satisfied with the parental explanation of the recent
disappearance of a pet rabbit). *'Mummy, is–is this Gladys?'*

*'It was what I call classic music, if you know what I mean – not jazz.'*

# ARTHUR WATTS
## 1883-1935

Master of the bird's-eye view, Arthur Watts was one of *Punch*'s most distinctive and accomplished illustrators. Watts developed the perspective after renting an attic studio in Hampstead and claimed using the technique made it much more likely the cartoon would appear as a full page! He first contributed to the magazine in 1912; after a break during WWI and his subsequent recovery from shell-shock, Watts' work began appearing again in 1921 until his untimely death in a plane crash in 1935.

Arthur Watts, 1934

**THE FALSE NOTE**

Arthur Watts, 1927

*Our vicar's wife buys a new hat.*

**MODERN SIGHTSEEING.**

"Salisbury Cathedral! The highest spire in England!"

Arthur Watts, 1933

Arthur Wallis Mills, 1934

'I didn't know you'd ever taken that car abroad.' 'As a matter of fact
I haven't, but I do get some attention now.'

Kenneth Beauchamp, 1934

'What would you say if you was me if he says what he says he's going to say?'

William Leigh Ridgewell, 1934

**HOSPITALITY; OR THAT CHRISTMAS FEELING**

Frank Reynolds, 1934

Small autograph-hunter. *'Have you got Bradman?'*
Smaller autograph-hunter. *'No, but I've got the signature of
a chap that has.'*

Pont (Graham Laidler), 1937

**THE BRITISH CHARACTER**
*Patience*

Hostess. *"Instead of our usual servants' ball this year I've invited the staff to come up here to watch our Bridge."*

*'You see, Auntie, then I could drive it for you.'*

Frank Reynolds, 1934

Host. *'Now perhaps you understand, old man, why I never want
to hang about town when we've finished at the office.'*

George Sherriff Sherwood, 1934

*'I've tested this new drill, sir. It seems to be all right.'*

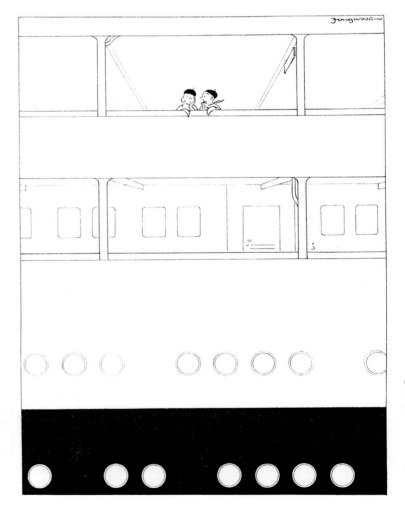

Fougasse (Kenneth Bird), 1934

- 177 -

*'I may not be able to get ashore tomorrow to see Pompeii.
There's some talk of holding the final of the deck-billiards.'*

Pont (Graham Laidler), 1934

**THE BRITISH CHARACTER**
*Skill at foreign languages.*

Paul Crum (Roger Pettiward), 1938

*'I expect you knew this place
when it was a snipe bog?'*

George Sherriff Sherwood, 1935

**THE GARDEN SEASIDE!**
*Great fun! Complete in box, with breeze-creator, paddling pan,
pebbles, seaweed, crab, starfish, etc.*

Harry Hewitt, 1938

'Listen, Vera—who is driving this car,
you or your mother?'

Douglas Lionel Mays, 1935

'Come – don't dawdle, Eustace.'

James Henry Thorpe, 1933

'Apart from all the modern advantages, madam, you have
here an exact replica of an Elizabethan maisonette.'

*'No, we don't speak French, but when we're in France
we speak our own language but with a foreign intonation.'*

*'You're his friend—you tell him.'*

**THE BRITISH CHARACTER**
*Importance of tea.*

**THE HEIRESS FALLS OVERBOARD.**

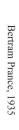Bertram Prance, 1935

Pont (Graham Laidler), 1935

'NEWS.'

Fougasse, 1937

Fougasse (Kenneth Bird), 1935

Edgar Norfield, 1937

'...and finally I discovered a silly error
of my own, Mr Bartram.'

William Augustus Sillince, 1937

'Yes, the Duke and I had one hell of a row this morning.'

George Morrow, 1935

'Try and get a good one of Bimbo. He remembers me since my last visit.'

David Louis Ghilchik, 1932

Client (to solicitor). 'So I said to them, 'I've tried to get a settlement by fair means and failed. You will now hear from my lawyer.'

George Sherriff Sherwood, 1934

*Unfortunate position of skater when only passer-by was a Fascist.*

Pont (Graham Laidler), 1935

**THE BRITISH CHARACTER.**
*Love of writing letters to The Times.*

W Heath Robinson, 1936

**FLAT-LIFE.**
*The Bird-Bath.*

# FOUGASSE 1887-1965
## KENNETH BIRD

The art directors' favourite, the unique stylish shorthand of Kenneth Bird's drawings seem to epitomise the period between the World Wars. His pen name 'Fougasse' came from a type of land mine of unreliable explosiveness. Art editor of *Punch* from 1937, Bird was appointed editor in 1949 – the only cartoonist to hold the post. He updated the look of the magazine and nurtured a new generation of cartoonists. Outside *Punch*, Fougasse was best-known for the cartoons he drew for *Careless Talk Costs Lives*, the series of propaganda posters produced by the Ministry of Information during the Second World War.

1936

'Anyway, I wouldn't take the girls to it till you've seen it yourself.'

1936

'No, the news isn't worse than usual this morning— but the crossword is.'

Fougasse (Kenneth Bird), 1951

'That reminds me dear—did you remember the sandwiches?'

"WOULD YOU HAVE THE GOODNESS TO STOP TALKING, SIR?'
"I WAS *NOT* TALKING, SIR."
"WELL, YOU ARE NOW, ANYWAY."

Fougasse (Kenneth Bird), 1927

Bertram Prance, 1930

Motorist. *'I'm afraid we've knocked him silly.'*
Wife. *'Don't go giving him a lot of money, dear. Perhaps he's the village idiot.'*

David Louis Ghilchik, 1936

*'I won't be home to-night, Mums, but everything's quite all right—I've been arrested.'*

Edgar Spenceley, 1936

*'I wish you'd never bin to that there Ideal 'Ome Exhibition.'*

John G Walter, 1936

*'No, I couldn't get the shipping forecast—not without cutting into the symphony from Stuttgart.'*

Pont (Graham Laidler), 1936

**THE BRITISH CHARACTER**
*Enthusiasm for gardening.*

George Belcher, 1936

Lodgekeeper. *'Very sorry, sir, we don't allow no picknickers any more. They used to throw bread at the swans and other hacts of Bolshevism.'*

Henry Mayo Bateman, 1932

**THE HIGH PRIESTESS**

Fougasse (Kenneth Bird), 1936

*'Is that the telephone?' 'Yes, madam.'
'What does it want?'
'It wants you to lunch with it on
Tuesday, madam.'*

Pont (Graham Laidler), 1936

## THE BRITISH CHARACTER
*Love of detective fiction.*

James Henry Thorpe, 1936

*'Racing's like that, my dear. You win one
day and lose the next.'*
*'Why not come every other day, uncle?'*

David Louis Ghilchik, 1936

*'Of course I'm only a woman, but I don't see what good it does
the country having a budget. It only means worrying before you
spend the money instead of after.'*

George Sherriff Sherwood, 1936

TO GET THE BEST RESULTS, CRAZY PAVING SHOULD *ALWAYS* BE LAID BY CRAZY PAVIORS.

Pont (Graham Laidler), 1936

**THE BRITISH CHARACTER**
*The attitude towards fresh air.*

Lewis Baumer

*'Don't worry, darling, you'll look quite respectable in a day or two.'*

Pont (Graham Laidler), 1936

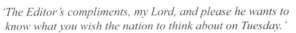

'The Editor's compliments, my Lord, and please he wants to
know what you wish the nation to think about on Tuesday.'

Fougasse, 1936

*A cricketer has just retired from active
participation in the game owing to
increasing weight. We understand that
he is shaping very well as an umpire.*

Treyer Evans, 1928

'I can't come out yet, dear; I'm washing the baby.'

Fougasse (Kenneth Bird), 1936

'So you've got some guests already?'
'No—them's just decoys.'

Kenneth Beauchamp, 1936

'Have we a copy of Karl Marx? Well, the children are sure to have one up in the nursery.'

*Lewis Baumer, 1932*

*In view of the fact that we go to press before Bank Holiday, our artist thought it wiser to supply enough illustrations under the above heading to cover all probable contingencies. In the unlikely event of the day being fine, readers will kindly consider this page a wash-out.*

Futurist painter (delightedly). *'I've sold this one, Mrs Biggs.'* Landlady. *'Us ought to go shares then. Some o' them smudges I did when I was 'avin' a dust round.'*

*'We must on no account permit anyone to give us a shock, Mr. Pembridge. The least shock of any sort would in our present state of health be sure to kill us immediately.'*

'Now, sir, your father don't pay £300 a year in school fees to
have you flicking at balls just outside the off stump.'

James H Thorpe, 1937

'Fish here much?' 'Yes.' 'What for?' 'Bream mostly.' 'What size?'
'Anything up to five pounds.' 'What they look like?' 'I've no idea.'

Fougasse (Kenneth Bird), 1937

Charles Grave, 1934

**GETTING USED TO US**
'Look at 'em! Now wouldn't you 'ave thought they would all 'ave bin
excited an' 'appy at seein' English visiters?'

Pont (Graham Laidler), 1936

**THE BRITISH CHARACTER**
*Strong tendency to become doggy.*

George Sherriff Sherwood, 1933

Wife. *'You and I are comin' to the cross-roads, Arnold; That's twice you've been out without remembering to buy the canary-seed.'*

Paul Crum (Roger Pettiward), 1937

*'I'm not wild about that the hat. Couldn't you wear something more non-committal?'*

Reginald Cleaver, 1937

*'It is true, me lud, that my client threw a bottle of wine at the defendant's head. But I submit, me lud, that it was a very light wine, and, in fact, a wine that couldn't possibly hurt anybody.'*

- 200 -

Fougasse, 1936

*'Is this the way to W—A—R—E—H—A—M?'*

Pont (Graham Laidler), 1937

**THE BRITISH CHARACTER**
*Partiality for open fires*

Arthur Wallis Mills, 1934

*'Her Ladyship has joined the League of Youth and Beauty and begs you to
excuse her for a few minutes while she finishes her exercises.'*

Arthur Wallis Mills, 1933

Scion of an ancient house. *'I am fed-up with all this sham. I'm joining the Communist Party.'*
Fiancée. *'Splendid of you, darling! But won't you have to live down your nose a bit?'*

Fougasse (Kenneth Bird), 1937

*'Yes, madam—of course the other half of the staircase
goes with the maisonette below.'*

Pont, 1937

*'There are times when I really begin to
wonder if all this is worth while.'*

Pont (Graham Laidler), 1937

- 203 -

**THE BRITISH CHARACTER**
*Love of keeping calm.*

Fougasse (Kenneth Bird), 1937

*'This is our latest novelty—a writing-desk that turns out to be a wireless-set.' 'There's nothing much new in that.' 'Ah, but this is a writing-desk that tuns out to be a wireless-set that turns out to be a cocktail cabinet that turns out to be a writing-desk after all.'*

'I wonder if it's worth seeing?'

Pont (Graham Laidler), 1934

Bert Thomas, 1934

First angler. 'I can't find that fish I caught.'
Second angler. 'I think you put it in your cigarette-case.'

Frank Reynolds, 1937

Horribly successful batswoman. *'Never you mind 'ow I 'olds it—*
*you ain't got me out yet!'*

*'Hullo!—Yes?!—Yes?!!—*

*Yes?!!!—Who is it?!!!!—*

*Who is it?!!!!!—*

*Oh...it's you...*

*My dear, how perfectly delightful to*
*hear your voice!!!'*

Fougasse (Kenneth Bird), 1937

Lewis Baumer, 1937

**THE NATIVES**

Pont (Graham Laidler), 1937

**THE BRITISH CHARACTER**

*A tendency to put things away safely*

George Loraine Stampa, 1933

Father. *'Well, wot did they learn yer at Sunday School?'* Betty. *'That I'm a child of Satan.'*

George Belcher, 1939

'Nobody not on the menu ain't allowed inside the barrier.'

Fougasse (Kenneth Bird), 1937

'Now, quick! Shall we say we were kept by a long
telephone call as we were leaving home, and knew
they'd understand, or shall we pretend we thought they
said half-past eight, which is virtually the truth?'

Pont, 1937

'I wonder if there's a really nice little boy
in the room who would like to run upstairs
and look for Mummy's spectacles!'

# HOLIDAYS

The summer holiday flourished in the Victorian Era as the rapidly expanding railways made Britain's coasts accessible and the great British seaside holiday was born – for the prospering middle classes at least. But by the end of the nineteenth century the working classes flocked to the beaches, too. The sunbathing craze and camping reflected a post WWI interest in health and fresh air, and while the working classes travelled en masse to crowded resorts, the middle classes were moving further afield to the Continent.

*The poster invited us —*

*so we went.*

Arthur Wallis Mills, 1937

Arthur Watts, 1924

Fond wife (whose husband has gone to the farm for supplies).
*'The opening's on this side, darling.'*

John Leech, 1857

**A JUDGE BY APPEARANCE**
Bathing guide. *'Bless 'is 'art! I know'd he'd take to it kindly—
by the werry looks on 'Im!'*

Pont (Graham Laidler), 1936

**THE BRITISH CHARACTER**
*Absolute indispensability of bacon and eggs for breakfast.*

Douglas (Douglas England), 1937

**THE BRITISH CHARACTER.**
*Importance of not being intellectual.*

Pont (Graham Laidler), 1937

Paul Crum (Roger Pettiward), 1938

*'He's only tolerated on
account of his rice-puddings.'*

Frank Reynolds, 1937

*'This be the wickut, mister, when oi've give 'er the once-over!'*

Lewis Baumer, 1937

'But you're very young, Jane. You are not thinking of getting
married to him yet?' 'Oh, no, m'lady—not for years. It would
leave so long afterwards, wouldn't it, m'lady?'

Fougasse, 1937

'And what might your name be? Prudence?'

Hamilton Williams, 1935

'Another sunny week-end! Let's let the encyclopaedia
slide and pay the instalment on the car!'

Pont (Graham Laidler), 1937

- 213 -

**THE BRITISH CHARACTER.**
*A regard for good tailoring.*

David Langdon, 1937

'I'm not sure, Sir, but I believe I've split the atom.'

Paul Crum (Roger Pettiward), 1937

'It's so difficult to look as if one was doing it for a
joke without looking as if one was enjoying it.'

Paul Crum (Roger Pettiward), 1937

'You ought to be stamping out crime
somewhere, not just standing there.'

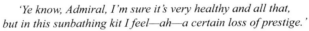

Arthur Wallis Mills, 1935

'Ye know, Admiral, I'm sure it's very healthy and all that,
but in this sunbathing kit I feel—ah—a certain loss of prestige.'

Lewis Baumer, 1937

'But of course, darling, any fiancé of yours is more than welcome.'

George Loraine Stampa, 1937

*'Garge, you and I be coorting now for nigh on ten
year, it's 'bout time we thoort o' getting wed.'*
*'Aye, lass, but 'oo would 'ave us now?'*

Fougasse (Kenneth Bird), 1937

- **215** -

*'There! That time I got right across without hitting anything.'*

David Louis Ghilchik, 1937

*'Ah, this must be my husband. I recognise some of the parcels.'*

Arthur Wallis Mills, 1937

'Why not wear your Fascist uniform, Walter?
They couldn't say anything as it's fancy-dress.'

George Whitelaw, 1938

'And what did you do in the Ice Age, Grannie?'

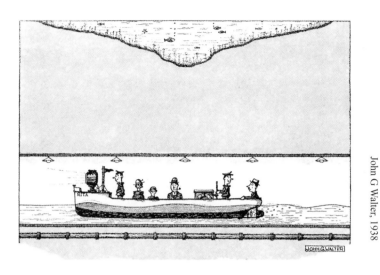

John G Walter, 1938

'Oh yes, sir, the ferry and subway companies
amalgamated some time ago.'

William Bird (Jack Butler Yeats), 1938

**CONVERSATION PIECE.**
'I dreamt I met Napoleon last night.'  'What was he like?'
'Enthusiastic.' 'What about?' 'He didn't say.'

- 217 -

Pont (Graham Laidler), 1938

'Bring her another duck, waiter.'

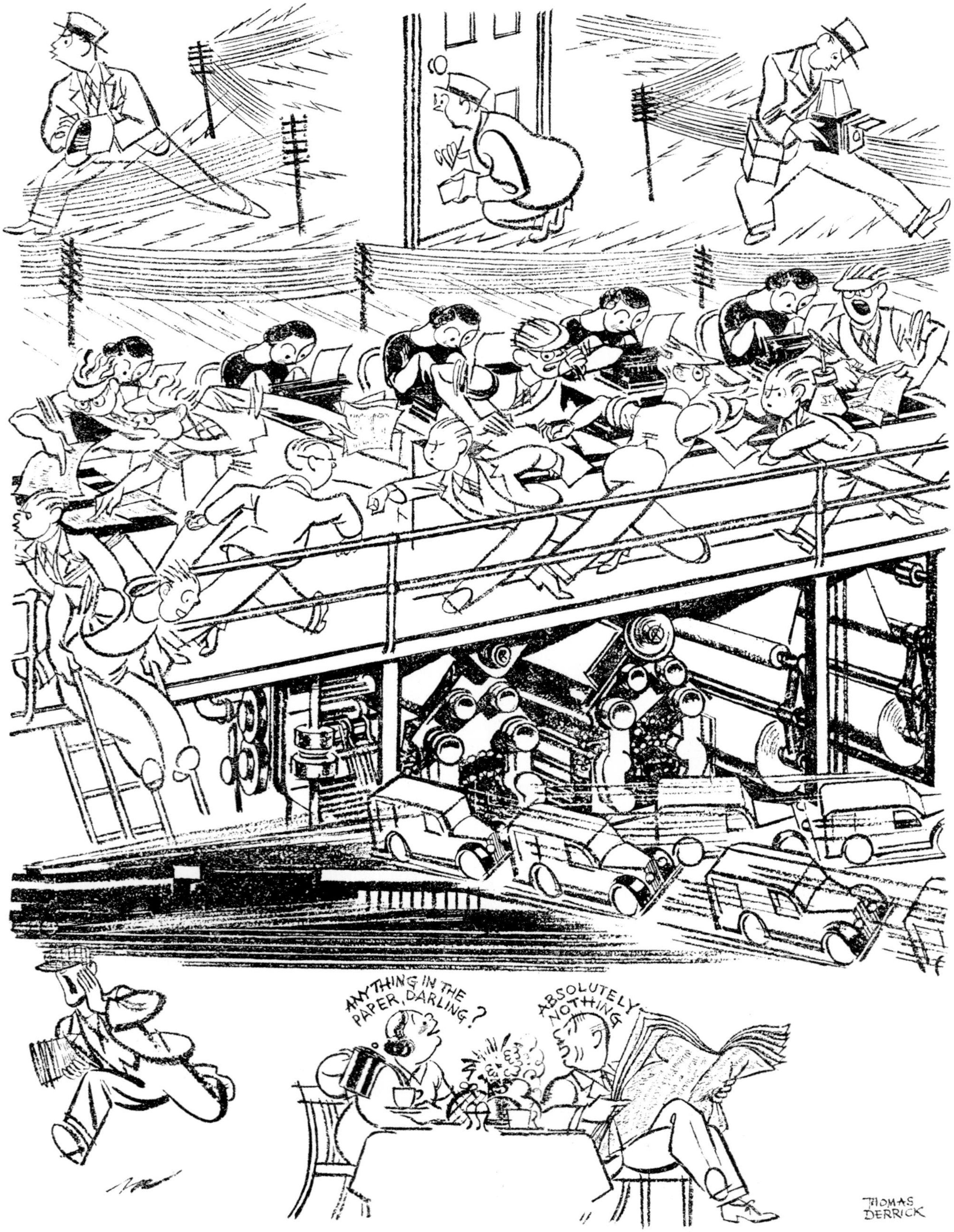
ANYTHING IN THE PAPER, DARLING?
ABSOLUTELY NOTHING
THOMAS DERRICK

NEWS

Derrick, Thomas, 1938

Pont (Graham Laidler), 1938

'Miss Sylvia asked me to inquire, your Ladyship, whether she need wash this morning in view of her having taken a bath only yesterday evening.'

Lewis Baumer, 1927

'By the by, when does your divorce come off?' 'End of October. Of course we'd love to see you, but we're only asking relatives.'

Lewis Baumer, 1938

'Do go and get my library book, darling—it's up in my bedroom.' 'What's the
title?' 'I'm not absolutely certain, but I think it's called 'Men are so Helpless.''

Pont, 1938

'Master George would
prefer rice-pudding.'

Brian Robb, 1938

'Veal's off, sir; Chops is off, and, unless
my nose deceives me, duck's off too.'

Paul Crum (Roger Pettiward), 1938

'I don't suppose that group means anything to
you, but it happens to be Serge Lifar
on my left and Picasso behind.'

John G Walter, 1938

'The natives used to call it 'The Mighty Hill
of Paradise that meets the moon,' but I've
renamed it 'Mount Emily Louisa Bagthorpe,'
after an aunt of mine.'

Alan Hervey d'Egville, 1938

'May I ask you to be a witness, sir?'
'Rather! What happened?'

Pont (Graham Laidler), 1938

**THE BRITISH CHARACTER**
*Ability to be ruthless*

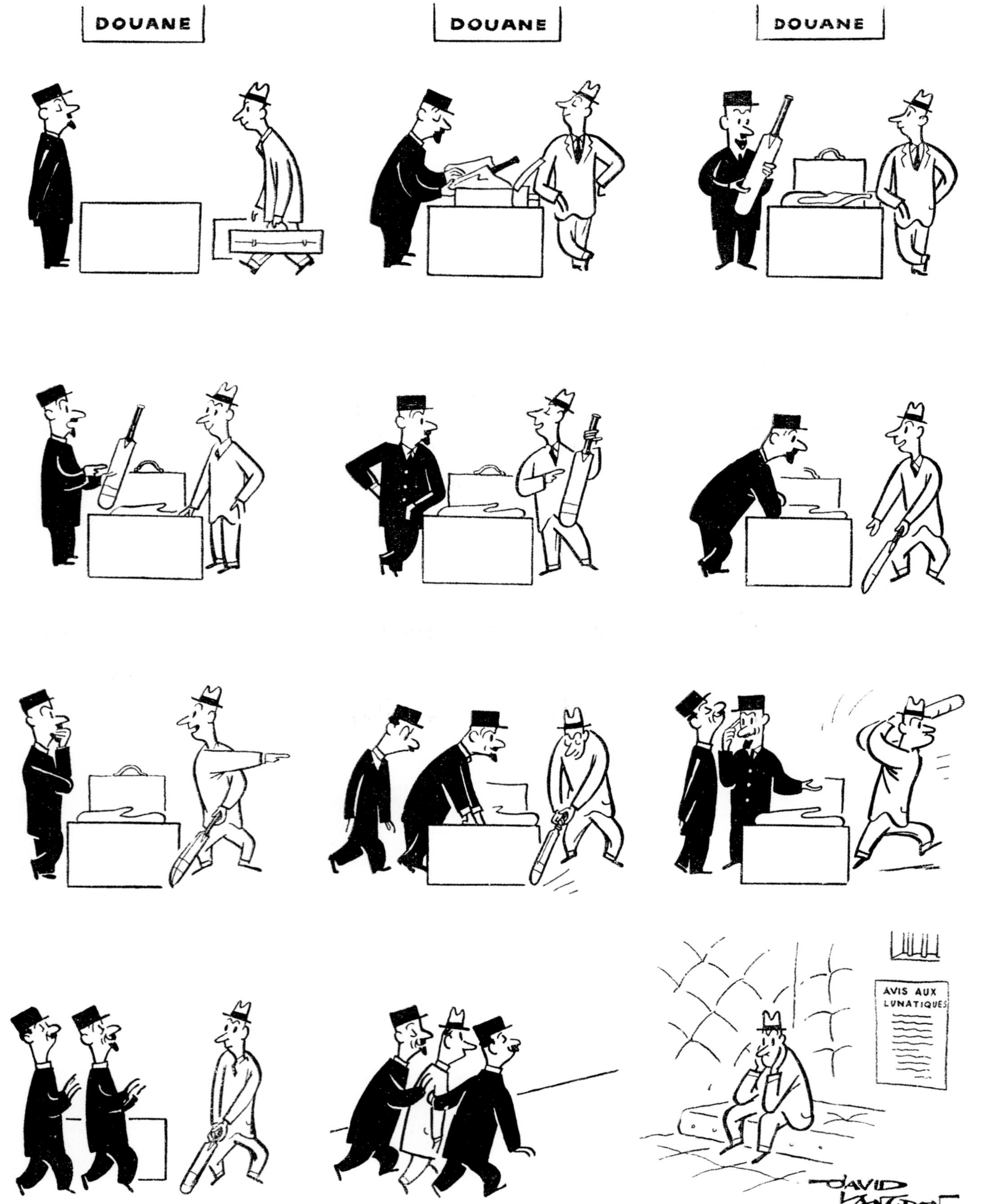
DOUANE
DOUANE
DOUANE
AVIS AUX LUNATIQUES
DAVID LANGDON

David Langdon, 1939

George Loraine Stampa, 1939

'I can't serve you.'
'Well, fetch the bloke as can.'

John G Walter, 1938

- 223 -

'Well, we're certainly lucky; Conditions are just
about ideal for a great forward battle.'

Pont, 1939

'Good heavens, Mother,
what have you been doing
with your hair?'

Arthur Wallis Mills, 1934

'I hear your dear wife is to give our Women's Institute a lecture.'
'My dear lady, it's no use appealing to me. I can't stop her.'

Harold William Hailstone, 1938

'Good, sir? Why, it's changed my 'ole outlook on life.'

William Augustus Sillince, 1938

'I wouldn't go round saying 'Salaam, Hitler!''

Pont, 1937

*'And now Mother's very cross indeed with you!'*

Paul Crum (Roger Pettiward), 1937

*'I keep thinking it's Tuesday.'*

Pont (Graham Laidler), 1938

**AT HOME**
*The cricket enthusiast*

Brian Robb, 1938

'Shall we lead them astray?'

John Whitfield Taylor, 1939

'I wish you'd mentioned,
Miss Titterton, that you've got rhythm.'

Pont, 1939

'I thought we might weed the paths today, Brown.'

Pont (Graham Laidler), 1938

**AT HOME**
*The singer*

H W Murray, 1939

*'This is a frightful party and I've a splitting headache.'*

David Langdon, 1938

*'He keeps on saying 'science knows no frontiers'—
and he hasn't a passport.'*

Arthur Wallis Mills, 1939

'All very fine for you, Dad, you've retired. You just try living in 1939.'

David Langdon, 1939

'I'm afraid we'll have to take that phobia right out
of the subconscious, Mr. Wainwright.'

Fred Pegram, 1937

*'Now, your grandfather, 'e were a proper gentleman. E'd come into the
garden of a mornin' and take no more notice of me than if I were a worm.'*

Lewis Baumer, 1939

*'Would Moddom care to try our 'not-quite-so-slim, not-quite-so-young' salon?'*

Pont (Graham Laidler), 1938

'Sir Thomas and Lady Partingdale, Lord Crodleigh and the Bishop of Hopton.'

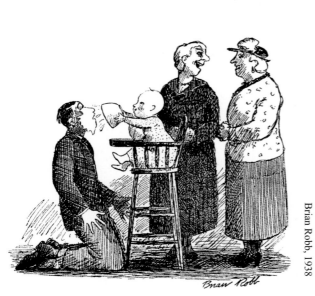

Brian Robb, 1938

'We call that the porridge game.'

Arthur Wallis Mills, 1938

'Dessay there's summat to be said fur 'em.'

Leslie Illingworth, 1938

"Isn't it peaceful?"

# 1939–1945

## WORLD WAR TWO

Pont (Graham Laidler), 1938

'… I am begining to think I have been letting things worry me too much lately, because…'

John G Walter, 1939

'Well, it was your idea to have a black cat.'

William Augustus Sillince, 1939

'It's an old tradition in the Southern Skirmishers, Private Bideford-Dawlish, that when a sergeant says 'left turn' one turns to the left.'

David Langdon, 1939

'You can tell your teacher you don't want to be evacuated; last time you had it done you had a sore arm for a week, remember.'

App (Brian Appleby), 1939

Anton (Antonia Yeoman), 1940

'We think you ought to know, sir, that this particular model runs just as well on fizzy lemonade.'

*'Don't dance about on it, Winnie, you might fall through.'*

A.R.P. Dept. *'I feel sure
we could drive a fire-engine.'*

*'In Winklebury there's bags of sand but no
bags, while in Little Chipley there's bags
of bags but no sand.'*

*'As in the last war, Pendleby, the firm's policy will be 'Business as Usual'.'*

'And you've paid.'

' From down here I can see a chink
of light through your dining-room
curtains quite distinctly.'

'Funny—I've never seen that shop before.'

Anton (Antonia Yeoman), 1939

*'But apart from this, life is going on just the same as usual.'*

Paul Crum (Roger Pettiward), 1940

*'One misses a lot not understanding the lingo.'*

George Loraine Stampa, 1939

*'D-drive very carefully—I-I don't know how you'll see.' 'Oh, I never sees
anythink. I jest flies straight like a arrow—you'd be surprised.'*

## THE CHANGING FACE OF BRITAIN

### XIV.—ENGLISHMAN'S HOUSE

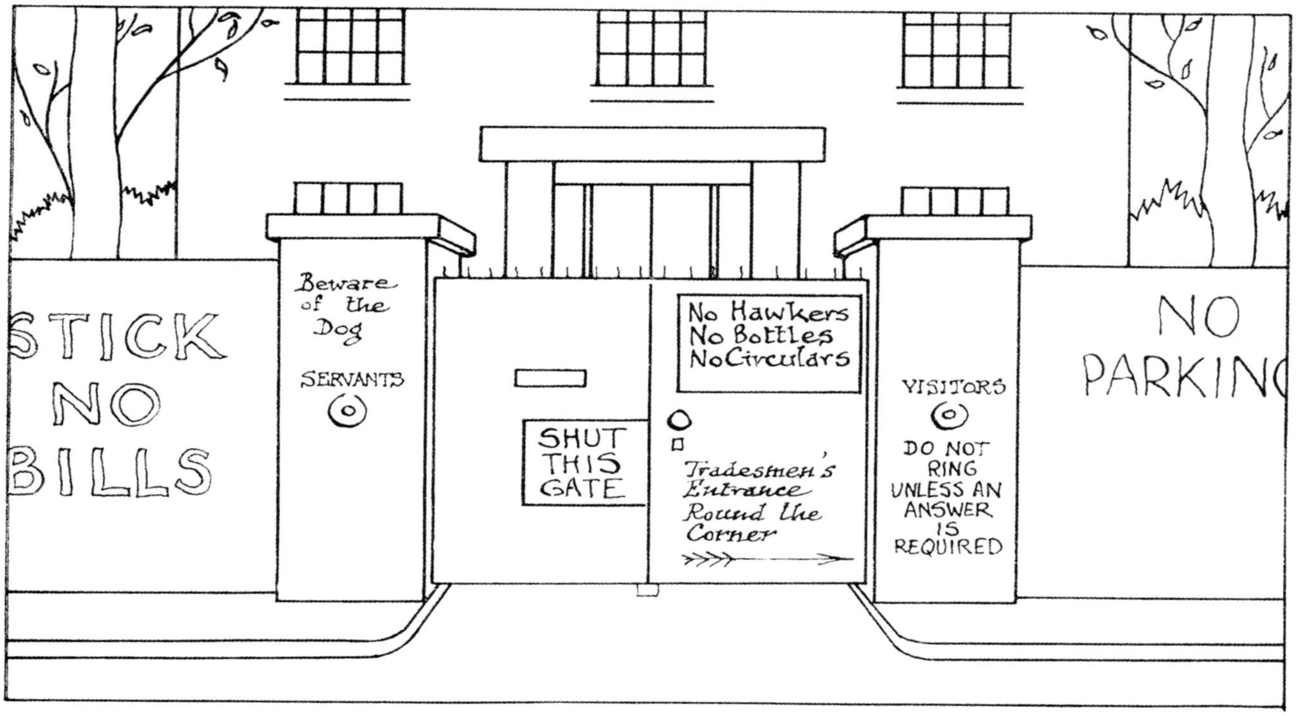
STICK NO BILLS
Beware of the Dog
SERVANTS
SHUT THIS GATE
No Hawkers No Bottles No Circulars
Tradesmen's Entrance Round the Corner
VISITORS
DO NOT RING UNLESS AN ANSWER IS REQUIRED
NO PARKIN

1

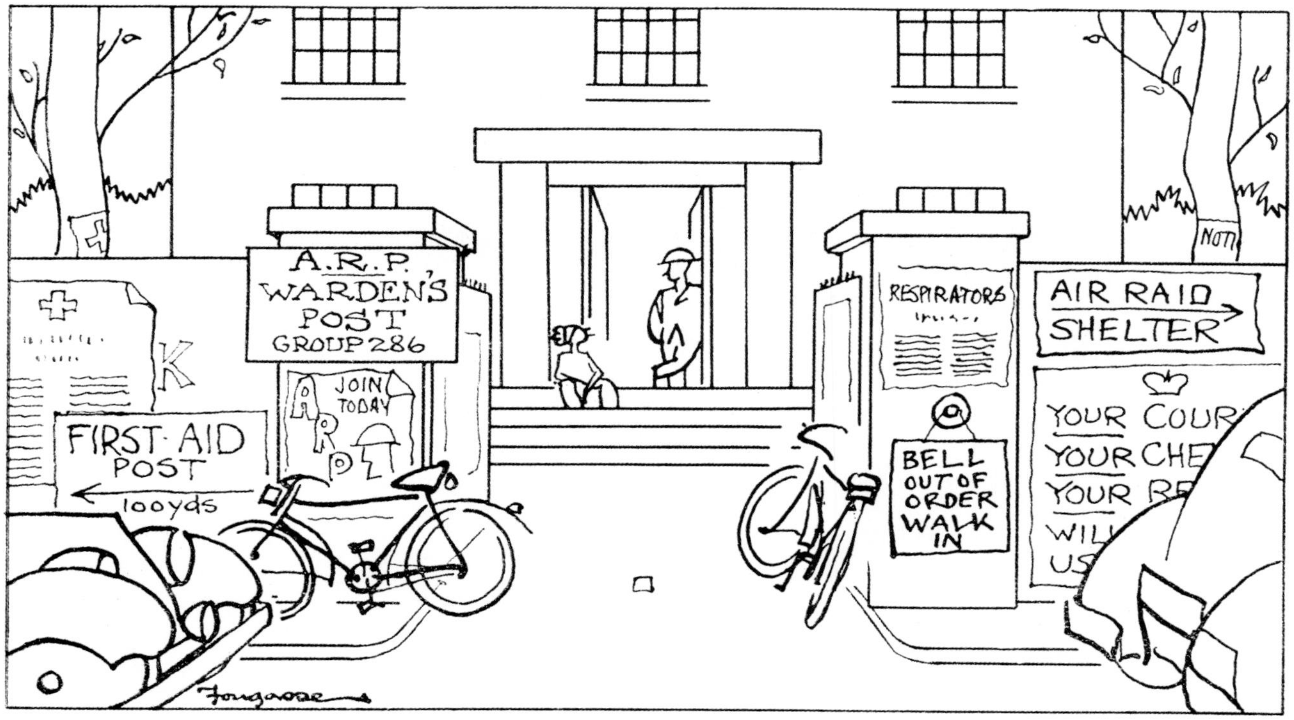
FIRST-AID POST
100yds
K
A.R.P. WARDEN'S POST GROUP 286
JOIN TODAY
A R P
RESPIRATORS
BELL OUT OF ORDER WALK IN
AIR RAID SHELTER
YOUR COUR
YOUR CHE
YOUR R
WIL
US
NOTI
Fougasse

2

Fougasse (Kenneth Bird), 1939

George Loraine Stampa, 1939

'I never know which is the 'tike cover' and which the 'all clear'; they sound
alike ter me—' specially if you've slep' through the 'tike cover.''

Pont (Graham Laidler), 1940

**POPULAR MISCONCEPTIONS**
*Life in the A.T.S.*

William Augustus Sillince, 1940

'It's no use getting fed up and wanting to go back to the house, John.
The first night we don't sleep in the shelter there's certain to be an air raid!'

Fougasse (Kenneth Bird), 1939

'Yes, that's for incendiary bombs – though I still don't
see why they aren't just as likely not to fall into it.'

John G Walter, 1940

'Do you think it's some sort of code?'

George Loraine Stampa, 1939

'Muvver says I don't need to bring my gas-mask, Miss, 'cause I ain't got no sense of smell.'

Lees, 1940

'Really, Mother, I keep telling you I don't need a chaperone.'

Pont (Graham Laidler), 1940

**POPULAR MISCONCEPTIONS (IN GERMANY)**
*The English*

George Adamson, 1940

*'...and this war will be won on the turnip-fields of Little Muggleton.'*

Ernest Howard Shepard, 1940

William Augustus Sillince, 1940

'Where will you 'ave the last couple o' sacks, lady? This 'ere air-raid shelter's full.'

Pont (Graham Laidler), 1940

**WAR-TIME WEAKNESSES**

*Seeing spies*

Pont, 1940

' I'm not going to have people turning
round and blaming me if we don't win
the damned war.'

David Langdon, 1940

'You should have laid more stress on the fact that
we were business evacuees.'

A McCulloch, 1941

- 243 -

'I wonder; can it be the one from number 44?'

Pont (Graham Laidler), 1939

**POPULAR MISCONCEPTIONS**
*Life in the B.E.F.*

William Augustus Sillince, 1940

'Yes, dear, it does help to keep one bright and cheerful these days.'

Hickey (George Hickson), 1940

'Miss Stapleton's been telling me how she won the last war by untying knots on parcels instead of cutting the string.'

Pont, 1940

' Come, come, Mr. Brewis, you aren't going to ration me!'

Paul Crum (Roger Pettiward), 1940

'Who was that foreign-looking fellow who
insisted on seeing the plans?'

Pont (Graham Laidler), 1939

' The men are complaining that the soup's
not as hot as it might be.'

Lewis Baumer, 1940

'Darling! Fancy your being in this war!'

William Augustus Sillince, 1940

'How on earth do you manage to keep your powder dry?'

Acanthus (Harold Frank Hoar), 1942

'I trust you benefited from last week's exercise in
unarmed combat.'

Leslie Baker, 1940

'I am instructed by the British Government to purchase
350 long-range heavy bombers, and by my wife to
purchase one "O-So-Handy" hair-drier.'

Harold William Hailstone, 1940

'...so I want you all to become even more potato-minded than usual.'

G E Moodey, 1940

'You'll have to take him—our coupons are inside.'

Pont (Graham Laidler), 1940

'Father, would not the best way to conduct the war be to let the editors of the newspapers take charge of it?'

*1.—Good news*

*3.—Worse news*

*4.—Definitely worse news*

*5.—Still worse news*

*6.—Bad news*

*2.—Not quite so good news*

Fougasse (Kenneth Bird), 1940

'But you must remember that I outnumbered them by one to three.'

'All right then, there is my identity card, birth
certificate and dog licence. And now, please,
am I right for Burbleton?'

'Now, if we're going to put this over properly,
you'll have to learn German.'

John G Walter, 1941

Frank Reynolds, 1940

'Yes, Major, but if this jungle is absolutely
impenetrable in all directions, how did we
manage to get to the middle of it?'

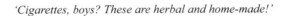

'Cigarettes, boys? These are herbal and home-made!'

George Morrow, 1940

'Council 'ave been and gone and filled 'e up, so I've reduced it to tuppence.'

- 251 -

*'Didn't you hear the warning?'*
*'Yes, thanks—but we can see quite well enough from here.'*

**WAR-TIME WEAKNESSES**
*Entertaining the troops*

*'Halt! Who goes there?...Halt!*
*Who goes there...Halt! Who goes there?'*

Hickey (George Hickson), 1940

'We're just a frying-pan short on this one.'

Pont, 1939

' ...' I remind you of who? ' I said.
And then I knocked the blighter down.'

William Augustus Sillince, 1940

'I'll have you leave the roller in the middle of the lawn in future,
Brown, in case any German aeroplane should attempt a landing.'

George Morrow, 1940

*'We can still see it, Mr Billinghurst.'*

Lawrie Siggs, 1942

Fougasse (Kenneth Bird), 1941

*'Dear Sirs, we regret that owing to changing
conditions in this topsy-turvy world...'*

*'What the blazes do you mean, 'After you, sir'?—
can't you see I'm only a private, confound you!'*

William Augustus Sillince, 1940

'And what have we done? We have allowed
ourselves to become the victims of mass hysteria!'

Hickey (George Hickson), 1940

'I've just discovered that we've been getting the
sirens mixed—darting in there at the continuous
blast and coming out again at the warbling note.'

Fougasse (Kenneth Bird), 1940

'Well, I must fly—or I shall be caught in the street by
the all clear, and then all the buses will be full.'

Harry Hewitt, 1940

" *Don't stand there knocking, Roberts,* GO STRAIGHT IN."

Hickey (George Hickson), 1940

*''I'm so sorry, young man. I'd no idea we'd
strayed into a military zone.'*

Pont, 1940

*' War of Nerves! War of Nerves! I haven't
the slightest idea what they mean.'*

- 256 -

William Augustus Sillince, 1941

*'Actually this is very much as Wren INTENDED us to see St. Paul's.'*

Fougasse (Kenneth Bird), 1940

*'Well, I found mine so horribly heavy on my head that I got my little dressmaker to copy it in felt.'*

David Langdon, 1943

*'Now in the ordinary way, if you came up against an obstacle like this, I dare say the tendency would be to go round it.'*

- 257 -

Frank Reynolds, 1941

*'Do you mind if we have the news on while you're telling us about your bombs?'*

Lawrie Siggs, 1941

David Langdon, 1940

'*Good evening, Madame. Over nine months ago –
on the 3rd of September, 1939, to be precise –
we declared war on Germany.*'

Pont, 1940

'*She's eating our butter.*'

Acanthus (Harold Frank Hoar), 1942

'I wish I could think of something to write home about.'

William Augustus Sillince, 1942

'Calm yourself, dear. Even Hitler can't be both dregs AND scum.'

'As your men have all been called up, we've been sent along to give you a bit of a hand.'

'I assume they'll be returned to me in good condition after the war.'

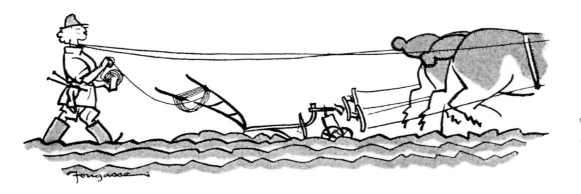

Norman Mansbridge, 1943

'Now we're all right, sir—here's our escort.'

Douglas Lionel Mays, 1941

'Take my seat, Miss—MADAM—SERGEANT.'

# SILLINCE 1906–1974
## WILLIAM AUGUSTUS SILLINCE

Sillince's career spanned advertising, teaching and television, but his work for *Punch* will be forever associated with the hundreds of wonderfully-drawn cartoons he contributed during the Second World War which captured so well the flavour and style of wartime Britain. One of the few *Punch* artists to produce their finished work in pencil, he used a carefully prepared canvas-grained paper that gave his cartoons their distinctive texture.

- 262 -

William Augustus Sillince, 1941

*'... and 'ere's me Identity Card, Lady.'*

William Augustus Sillince, 1937

*'Should we call him Spot?'*

William Augustus Sillince, 1941

'By the way, did you remember to feed the canary?'

William Augustus Sillince, 1937

'Garçon, this vin is extraordinarily ordinaire.'

William Augustus Sillince, 1942

'Officer, stop! What is the controlled price of onions?'

Norman Mansbridge, 1940

George Belcher, 1941

'We mustn't miss the six o'clock news, Annie.
I always consider it the most optimistic.'

David Langdon, 1941

'I'd like you to think up something catchy for the window, like 'Hitlers may come and Hitlers may go, but Murdoch and Wimpleby were established in 1783.''

Frank Reynolds, 1940

'Wuman, ye look tarrible!'

William Augustus Sillince, 1941

'Now, Miss Fforbes-Watson, have you had any experience of agricultural work?'

*George Loraine Stampa, 1941*

'*You'll have to be more careful, Mary, when you start handling sixteen-inch shells.*'

*William Augustus Sillince, 1942*

'*I'm afraid my coupons are loose—but I have brought witnesses who will give evidence that they are genuine and cut from my own ration-book.*'

*Mervyn Wilson, 1943*

*Fougasse, 1940*

'Here's a quite new sort of mystery story—
shortage of paper compelled the
publishers to omit the final chapter.'

'Yes, sir, I am aware that the posters say 'Freedom is in
peril, defend it with all your might'—nevertheless, I'm
afraid I can't let you pass along here without a permit.'

*Douglas Lionel Mays, 1941*

'...I've just met the sweetest young subaltern—and your car's had a collision with a tank.'

Harold William Hailstone, 1942

*'You want to go by the Elephant.'*

William Augustus Sillince, 1942

*'I wonder what's become of Mary?'*

Lawrie Siggs, 1942

'Now would be a good time to white-
wash his stall, Gladys.'

David Langdon, 1940

'19 Acacia Gardens still to come...'

Rowland Emett, 1942

*'I'm afraid business conditions won't allow us to raise your salary,
Miss Simpson, but as a slight token of their esteem the directors have
decided to present you with all their personal sweet coupons.'*

*'Next take a tablespoon of TNT....'*

*'Lucky? I'll say we were lucky!'*

Acanthus (Harold Frank Hoar), 1942

'They won't let on who the camp is for.'

Leonard Bradley Martin, 1942

'Well, we'd better go up to the enemy's position,
Arthur, and let them have a pot at him.

Frank Reynolds, 1942

'Look, Mummy! This is one they teach us!'

Lawrie Siggs, 1942

'No, they go down Laburnum Walk when they're going to Italy, and up Acacia Avenue when they're going to Germany.'

Pat Auld, 1942

'My wife, old man. She ran away to sea...'

Anton (Antonia Yeoman), 1940

'Listen—Stargazer says, 'To-day will be favourable to daring enterprise, and frontal attack will be the best strategy.''

Mervyn Wilson, 1942

'...and now, what is there I can buy to-day that you
won't have to-morrow?'

George Davies, 1942

'Now look fierce!'

Rowland Emett, 1942

SANDBAGS

THE
ABBEY RUINS
OF GREAT HISTORICAL
INTEREST.

GUIDE BOOK
OBTAINABLE FROM

NORMAN MANSBRIDGE

Norman Mansbridge, 1940

Douglas Lionel Mays, 1943

'There, darlings—you'd never guess what I made this of!'

Harold William Hailstone, 1943

'I don't mind telling you that this offence is
punishable with penal servitude, or even death, but
in view of your inexperience I shall just admonish
you and fine you the sum of ninepence.'

Lawrie Siggs, 1941

'I got my badge for incendiary bombs all right,
but I didn't do so well with HEs.'

*William Augustus Sillince, 1943*

*'How many more potatoes must I eat to sink a U-boat?'*

*Mervyn Wilson, 1942*

*'I understand you've been riveting in your name and address.'*

*Albert Edgar Beard, 1943*

*'But you're mistaken, dear—it's our night for sharing your fire!'*

'Pore lil' feller—I told Emily when she went into munitions that he'd never make a shopper.'

George Loraine Stampa, 1941

- 277 -

Acanthus (Harold Frank Hoar), 1942

'Shall we join the ladies?'

David Langdon, 1940

'Remember you used to say, why must I wear that silly little hat perched on the side of my head and I used to say, well, that's how they're worn?'

'Anyone in 'ere got any talent?'

'Isn't there a boy in the class who can draw a
different version of "Mary Had A Little Lamb"?'

'You just go back 'ome, Enery Tuppitt—all the village knows your
journey ain't necessary.'

# PAUL CRUM 1906-1942
## ROGER PETTIWARD

One of Pont's favourite cartoonists, Paul Crum's surreal humour was a precursor of today's off-the-wall cartooning. Crum gave *Punch* one of its best-loved and most remembered cartoons – 'I keep thinking it's Tuesday' (*see* page 225), with his two semi-submerged hippos musing in a pool. After Oxford and art studies in Vienna, Munich, Paris and London, Crum worked as an illustrator who was to have a lasting influence on other cartoonists. He was killed leading a Commando troop on a raid on Dieppe in 1942.

Paul Crum (Roger Pettiward), 1937

'Gosh! Are you P.K.'s Mater?'

Paul Crum (Roger Pettiward), 1936

'Well, which is it, Sam—a lovely old vase or a hideous modern one?'

Paul Crum (Roger Pettiward), 1937

'And lastly, never dispute the umpire unless you think he's wrong.'

Lawrie Siggs, 1943

*'I missed the swimming course, sergeant.'*

Mervyn Wilson, 1943

*'There's Rover with his wretched bone.'*

David Langdon, 1944

*'The usual guff about Sub-section
253, Allocation of Raw Materials
order, Board of Trade…'*

"*This is just to tell you, dearest Mabel, that you are the one and only girl in the whole world . . .*"

Fougasse (Kenneth Bird), 1943

Frank Reynolds, 1943

*'....So I said to him 'what you really need,' I said,
'is a sergeant to look after you."*

William Augustus Sillince, 1943

*'Now you'll remember that back in '40, when you 'adn't got weapons, you was
taught 'ow to use 'em. Well, this course in unarmed combat will teach you
'ow to get along without 'em now you've got plenty of 'em.'*

Lawrie Siggs, 1943

'What's the good of all these psychology tests if it only leads them to give me a job like this?'

Acanthus (Harold Frank Hoar), 1943

'There's not much doubt about the winner of this week's scrap metal drive.'

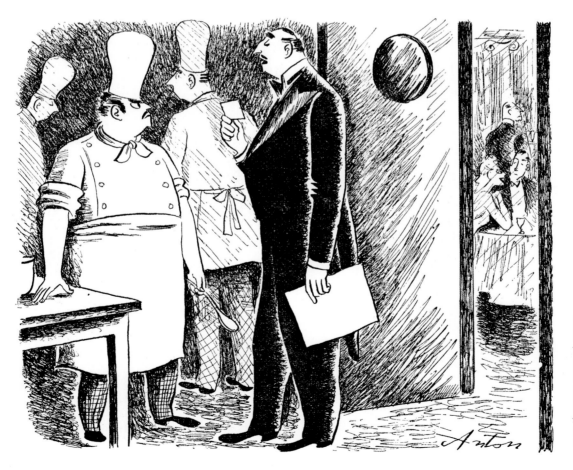

Anton (Antonia Yeoman), 1943

'A Mr Dixon of the Ministry of Supply's Synthetic Rubber Reasearch Department would very much appreciate your recipe for Crêpes Suzette.'

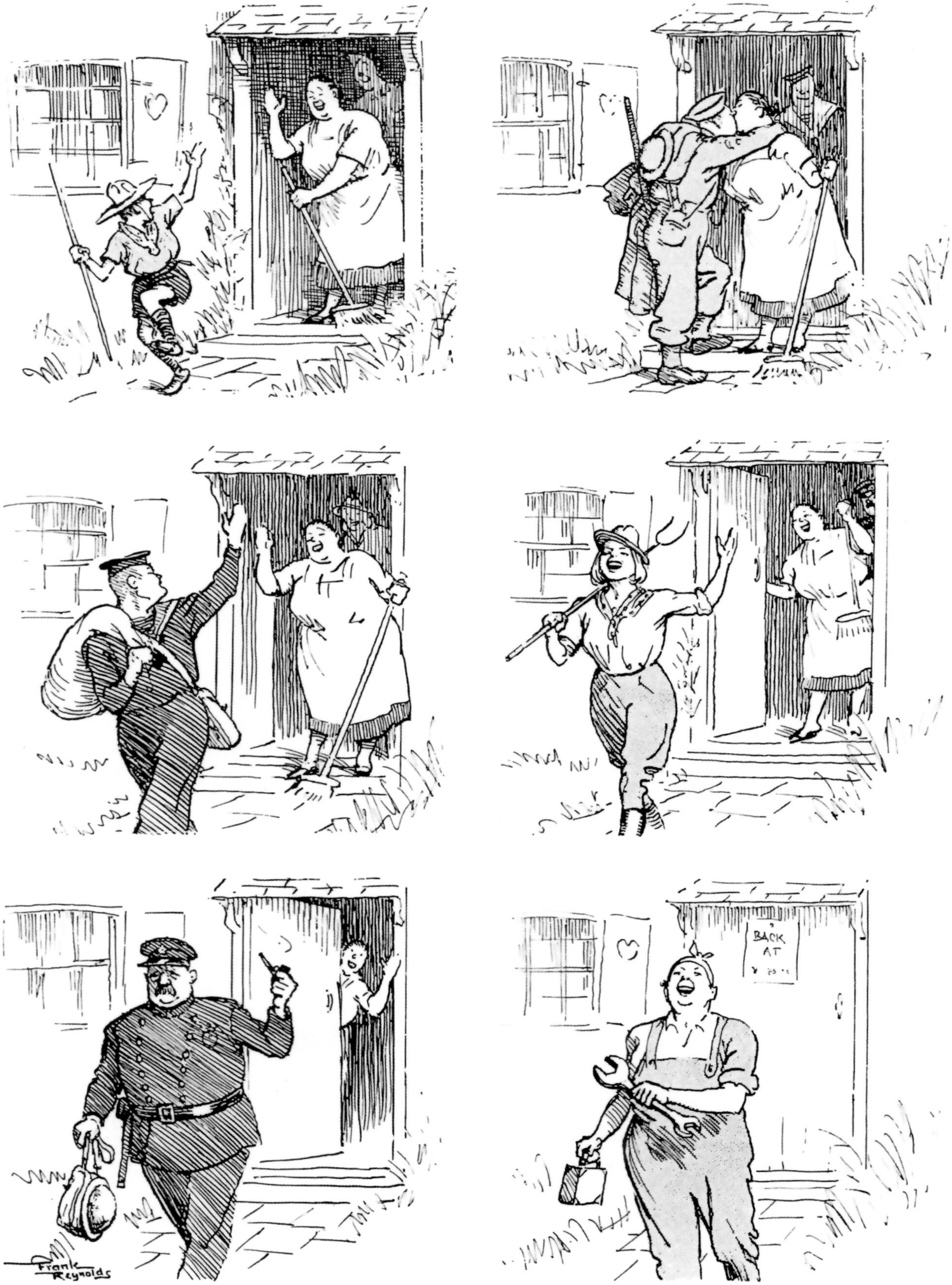
BACK
AT
Frank
Reynolds

Frank Reynolds, 1943

'This is Lieut Sienkiewics, sir; we call him Smith to distinguish him from
his friend Krzyianowski, who's known as Jones.'

'We might as well let Miss Daniells
have a holiday. I'm getting tired of
all these hints.'

'I'm goin' back—I've forgot me teeth!'
'Blimey! They're droppin' bombs, not sandwiches!'

William Augustus Sillince, 1944

*'My nephew's expecting to invade the continent very shortly.'*

Fougasse (Kenneth Bird), 1944

Frank Reynolds, 1944

*'I don't care if it is a special train for children evacuees,*
*Miss—you're not to announce it as a puff-puff.'*

Rowland Emett, 1944

'*They say, can we do two hundred and eighty-seven Dainty Afternoon Teas?*'

Maskee (W Beckett), 1944

'*Well, Mrs Tobin, if we make you a partner would you do the floor AND the windows?*'

Maurice Pownall, 1944

'*It appears these were the headquarters of the Hitler Youth.*'

Frank Reynolds, 1943

'... and finally, men, I want you to look on me as a father – if you have any
little troubles, bring them along to me.'

Acanthus (Harold Frank Hoar), 1943

'So, this is Oxford, the English Detroit.'

William Scully, 1944

'How many unreadable copies are we supposed
to type before we can change the ribbon?'

Mervyn Wilson, 1944

'Why shouldn't he sit there? Anyone would think
you had caught the rabbit.'

Fougasse (Kenneth Bird), 1944

David Langdon, 1944

'Anyone else in the class a gum-chum of
our American allies?'

William Augustus Sillince, 1945

'The old place hasn't changed a bit from 1917!'

Lawrie Siggs, 1941

'There you are, it's what I've always said—
anyone who had been sitting on the mantel-
piece would have been perfectly safe.'

Bernard Hollowood, 1944

NOTICE
5 INCHES

David Langdon, 1944

'Right! Now we've got that little lot off, what's the trouble with your bike?'

*Frank Reynolds, 1945*

*''Ere! 'Oo's supposed to be tellin' their experiences?'*

*Lawrie Siggs, 1942*

*'Gee, this is nothing—you ought to have seen the way we imagined it over in the States.'*

*Norman Mansbridge, 1944*

Anton (Antonia Yeoman), 1945

'I shall celebrate Victory-Day by switching over to asparagus.'

W. Mills, 1944

'If we hurry we should be able to capture it in
time for the nine o'clock news.'

David Langdon, 1944

'This week's subject for discussion is 'The World I Want After
the War.' Would someone please prod Gunner Tomkins sharply
in the ribs and ask him what sort of world he wants after the war.'

Anton (Antonia Yeoman), 1946

'...and this is my wife's little den.'

Maurice Pownall, 1946

'As you see, Peabody, your old job is still waiting for you.'

John Whitfield Taylor, 1946

'I'm afraid we're in for
another unsettled summer.'

*'I've an idea the professor's preoccupied with this brave new postwar-world business.'*

Rowland Emett, 1946

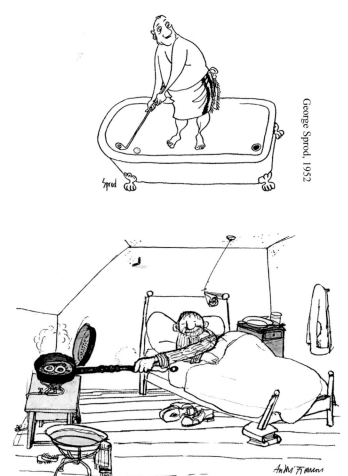

George Sprod, 1952

*'Yesterday it got down by itself.'*

Lawrie Siggs, 1946

André François, 1952

David Langdon, 1948

*'Tighten your belts everybody, please –
we're approaching Great Britain.'*

Anton (Antonia Yeoman), 1946

*'I was the Chairman of the Board until I found
out about the rates for overtime.'*

George Morrow, 1946

*'I picked him up at a sale of army surplus stores.'*

TO GREEN ROOM BAR

SANDWICHES · CAKES · PIES

Robert Stewart Sherriffs, 1951

**THE ACTORS' SYMPOSIUM**
(b) THE CELLULOID CAFETERIA

George Morrow, 1946

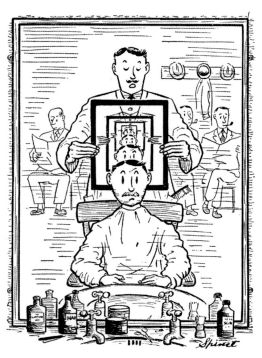

Bernard Hollowood, 1946

'*Another ha'penny on firelighters, Mr Mossley, and another regrettable step in the direction of uncontrolled inflation.*'

George Sprod, 1954

'*Oh Lord! Here he goes again.*'

Spinet (Roy Sackman), 1946

'*There you go, sir, travelling at the speed of light out into infinity.*'

Rowland Emett, 1946

Nicolas Bentley, 1955

'*Father, I want you to meet mother.*'

Dido (D M Brough), 1948

Douglas, 1946

Norman Thelwell, 1954

Henning Gantriis, 1955

Giovannetti, 1955

'I hid it.'

Harry Hargreaves, 1956

Anton (Antonia Yeoman), 1946

Michael ffolkes (Brian Davis), 1955

'*We're giving you a larger district, Johnson.*'

Bernard Hollowood, 1947

'*I don't see how you can
blame socialism for the thaw
AND the blizzard.*'

Kenneth Mahood, 1952

David Langdon, 1947

'*Have all your tickets, excess fares
and feeble excuses ready, please.*'

William Augustus Sillince, 1946

'*Good – Eric's settling down nicely in his new school.*'

Gerard Hoffnung, 1955

Frits Muller 1955

Acanthus (Harold Frank Hoar), 1946

Norman Mansbridge, 1946

'*It seems such a pity they have to grow up.*'

Mervyn Wilson, 1947

Alfred Jackson, 1952

Rowland Emett, 1946

'*You see they used to be in industry during the war.*'

Acanthus (Harold Frank Hoar), 1952

Bruce Petty, 1955

Anton (Antonia Yeoman), 1947

'Well, I'll marry you if you insist – but who do you suppose you're speaking to?'

Gerard Hoffnung, 1955

Smilby (Francis Wilford-Smith), 1955

Norman Thelwell, 1953

'*'Ow do they feel then?*'

John Whitfield Taylor, 1955

'*All right, Brannigan - we know you're in there!*'

Bernard Hollowood, 1947

'*And what are we supposed to do to this target – achieve it, surpass it, exceed it, go far beyond it, or just hit it?*'

# The Rake's Progress : The Novelist

RONALD SEARLE

**1. ADVENT** *Son of a North Country toiler. Writes authentic novel in dialect, on the backs of old envelopes between teabreaks.   Sacked*

**2. TRIUMPH** *Book published. Immediate Success. Acclaimed F*yles Literary Luncheon.  Mobbed in W·H·Sm*th's, Clapham*

**3. GLORY** *Second novel chosen as Book at Bedtime. Bats for Authors at National Book League Cricket match. Stage rights of 1st book bought for Wilfred Pickles*

**4. TEMPTATION** *Name unfamiliar to John Lehmann at P·E·N· Club party. Thenceforth tormented by desire to get into New Writing. Moves to Paris*

**5. DOWNFALL** *Critical analysis of J·P·Sartre rejected by London Magazine and Encounter. Sales of third novel sink to 750 copies ***

*\* Including British Commonwealth*

**6. RUIN** *Psychopathic treatment for schizophrenia. Emigrates to Australia.  Revered*

Ronald Searle 1954

Norman Mansbridge, 1947

'*Aston Villa, two; Blackburn Rovers, three...*'

David Langdon, 1949

'*'Ere we go again—the state versus free enterprise.*'

George Sprod, 1951

'*She's been immortalised by Mr. Wordsworth.*'

Anton (Antonia Yeoman), 1948

'*What a time I had persuading Mr Dali to paint the second one to match.*'

André François, 1947

Tim (William Timym), 1949

George Sprod, 1956

*'It's a little chilly, so I've put another dog on your bed.'*

Douglas, 1956

Gerard Hoffnung, 1955

Sheila Dunn, 1950

'*Order two sandwiches, then it doesn't matter whether they're masculine or feminine.*'

Walter Goetz, 1955

**- 311 -**

'*J'emmenerai le cocker, Jean—il va mieux avec mon nouveau tweed Anglais.*'

Anton (Antonia Yeoman), 1949

'*Don't give it a second thought – I'm always doing irreparable damage in other people's houses myself.*'

Lawrie Siggs, 1955

'*Next door seem to have started their holidays.*'

André François, 1949

Andri François

Mervyn Wilson, 1949

'*It's my wife – but there's probably some quite simple explanation.*'

Norman Mansbridge, 1949

'*What's up with you lately, old chap – is it some girl?*'

'The job holds excellent opportunities for a go-ahead man –
our last cashier got clear out of the country with
fifteen thousand pounds in negotiable bonds.'

'We're hoping that one day he'll remember his errand and
go off as mysteriously as he came.'

'The children just don't seem to confide in us any more.'

'Seems they had quite a party.'

# ROWLAND EMETT
## 1906-1990

E mett began contributing to *Punch* during the Second World War and his delicate
fantastical style soon began to evolve into the whimsical railways and eccentric
constructions that made his name. In 1951 he was invited to transform fantasy into
reality with the construction of the *Far Tottering and Oystercreek Railway* at the Festival of
Britain on London's South Bank. Emett became a household name and a new career began
creating the 'gothic-kinetic' machines that brought him fame in North America as well as
Britain; best-known was the car he created for the film *Chitty Chitty Bang Bang*.

Rowland Emett, 1946

'*Yes, there's always a certain amount of disturbance as
one actually goes through the sound barrier.*'

Rowland Emett, 1946

'*... Built by William the Conquerer, visited by
Queen Elizabeth, knocked down by Oliver
Cromwell, and restored by the Council for the
present occupier, Mr. 'Arry 'Iggins.*'

*'Between you and me, sir, we don't quite know where that line goes to.'*

Rowland Emett, 1946

Rowland Emett, 1946

*'Something to do with the nationalization of railways, I expect.'*

Russell Brockbank, 1955

'*Flyovers, motorways, and such! What's the
matter with the roads we've got?*'

Hickey (George Hickson), 1949

'*Now look here, Mulligan, I've had about
enough of your veiled insolence.*'

Anton (Antonia Yeoman), 1949

'*We'll leave this wall blank at the moment – in case
my husband shoots anything.*'

'*We want to know which of us has the inferiority complex.*'

'*Which vitamin is best for a deficiency in arithmetic?*'

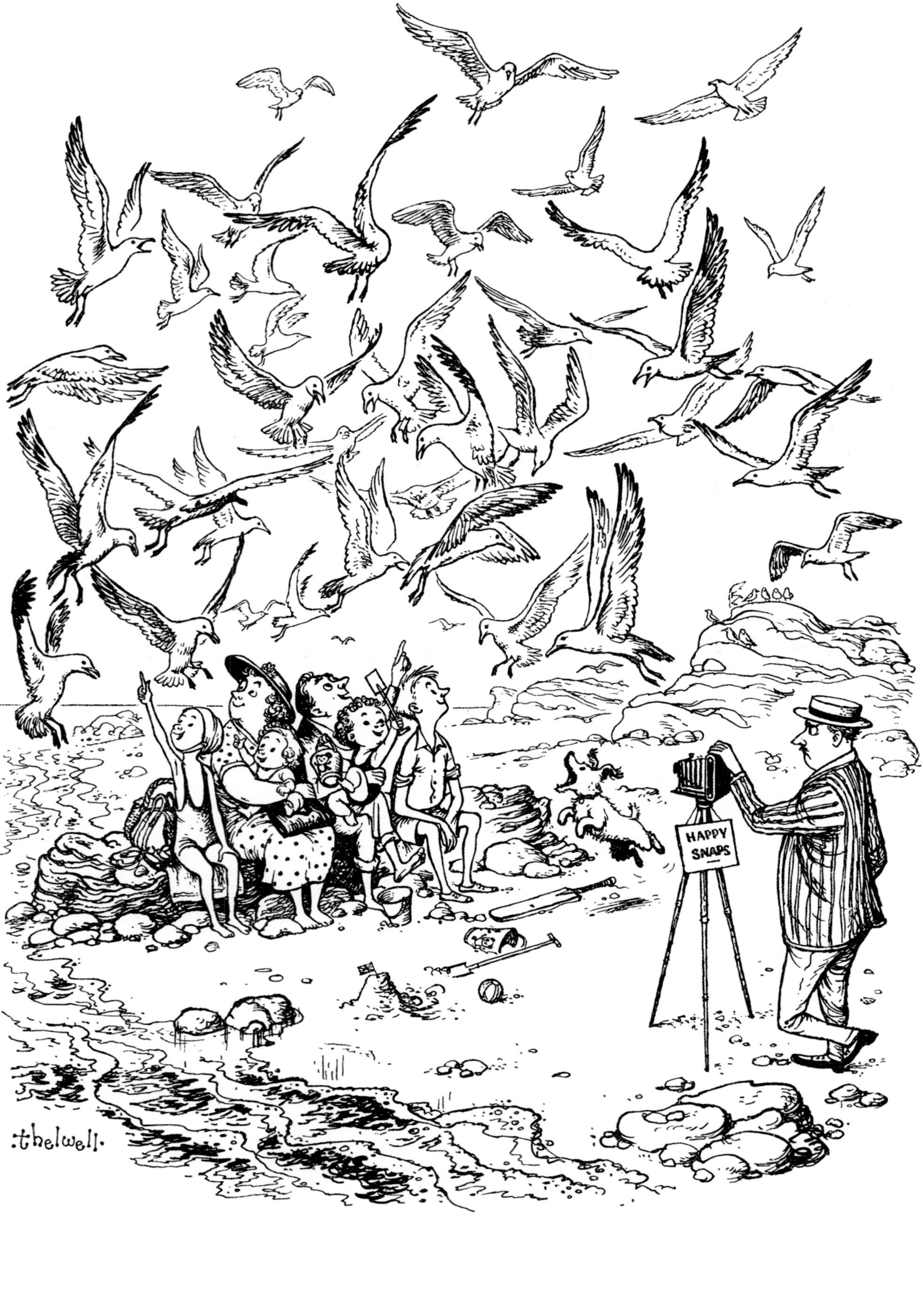
HAPPY SNAPS
thelwell

Norman Thelwell, 1954

'Isn't this where we take a thorn out of his foot or something?'

- 319 -

'I forgot the salt.'

George Sprod, 1949

Gerard Hoffnung, 1957

'One at a time, please, one at a time...'

Mervyn Wilson, 1949

'He doesn't know any tricks. he just sits there all day filling up football coupons.'

Harold William Hailstone, 1958

*'Ask yourself—what would Dan Archer do?'*

- 321 -

Lawrie Siggs, 1949

*'How do you mean, 'life is what you make it'?'*

Anton (Antonia Yeoman), 1952

Anton (Antonia Yeoman), 1950

'Once you've made the chalk mark, does that mean I've won?'

Gerard Hoffnung, 1957

RUNNING IN PLEASE PASS

DB 241

Russell Brockbank, 1950

George Sprod, 1955

Sheila Dunn, 1957

'*The roof garden was perhaps a mistake.*'

- 323 -

Michael ffolkes (Brian Davis), 1950

Henning Gantriis, 1951

'*Good heavens, Lavinia! It says here the East Wing was burned down last night.*'

Pericle Luigi Giovannetti, 1954

Anton (Antonia Yeoman), 1947

'*And to my faithful and devoted pets I leave the residue of...*'

Hickey, 1947

Douglas, 1957

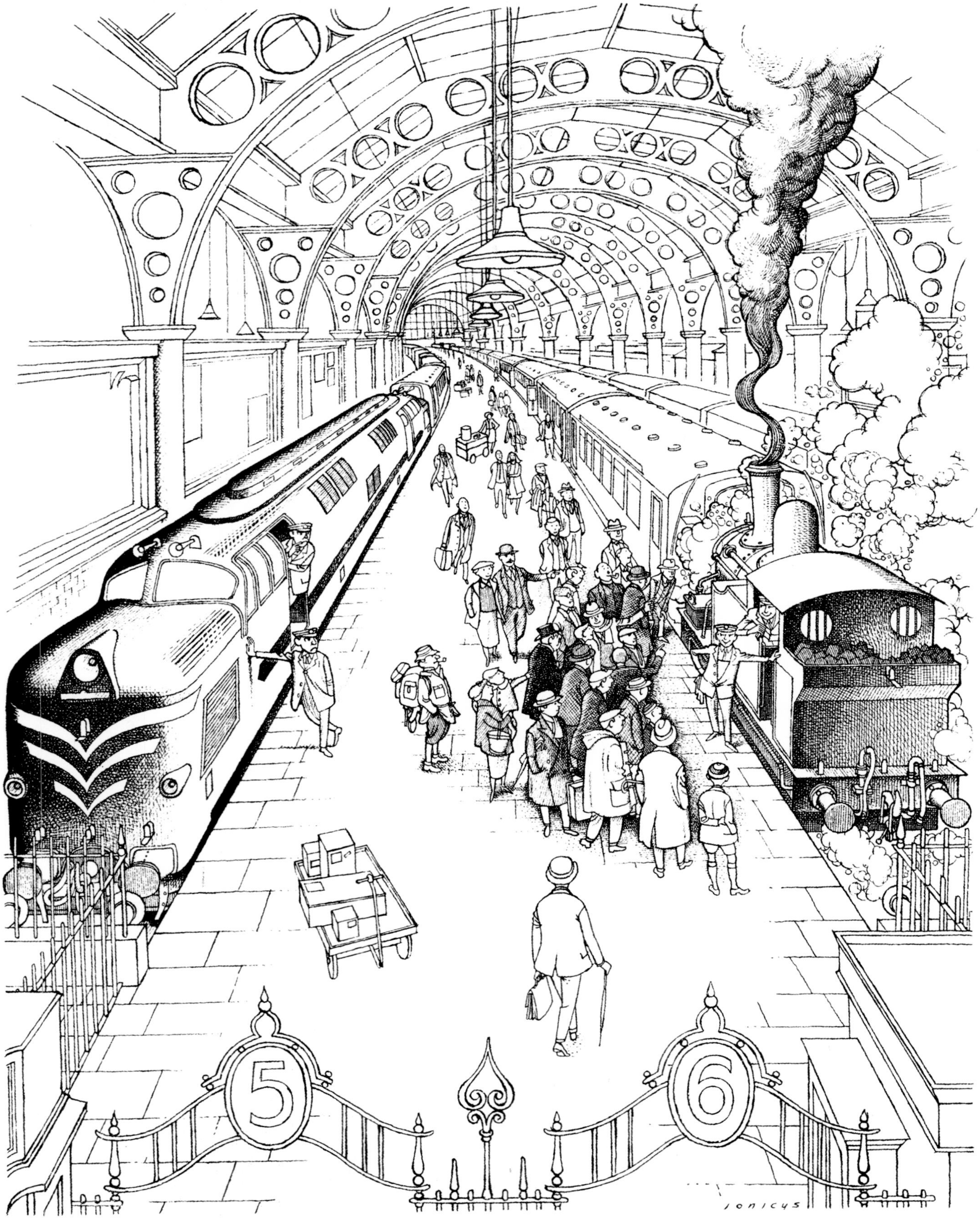
5
6
IONICUS

Ionicus (Joshua Armitage), 1957

John Whitfield Taylor, 1951

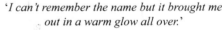

Michael ffolkes (Brian Davis), 1951

'*I can't remember the name but it brought me
out in a warm glow all over.*'

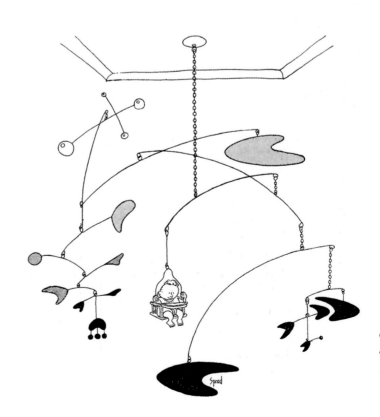

George Sprod, 1951

Norman Thelwell, 1952

'*Then, of course there'll be the usual search fee.*'

Maurice McLoughlin, 1951

'*The hanging committee seem to be
taking a stronger line this year.*'

Lawrie Siggs, 1951

'*What is it a sign of when a cow is lying down with
its four feet up in the air?*'

Rowland Emett, 1951

'*But Sir Bedivere always walks the battlements at this hour.
Can't think what's keeping him.*'

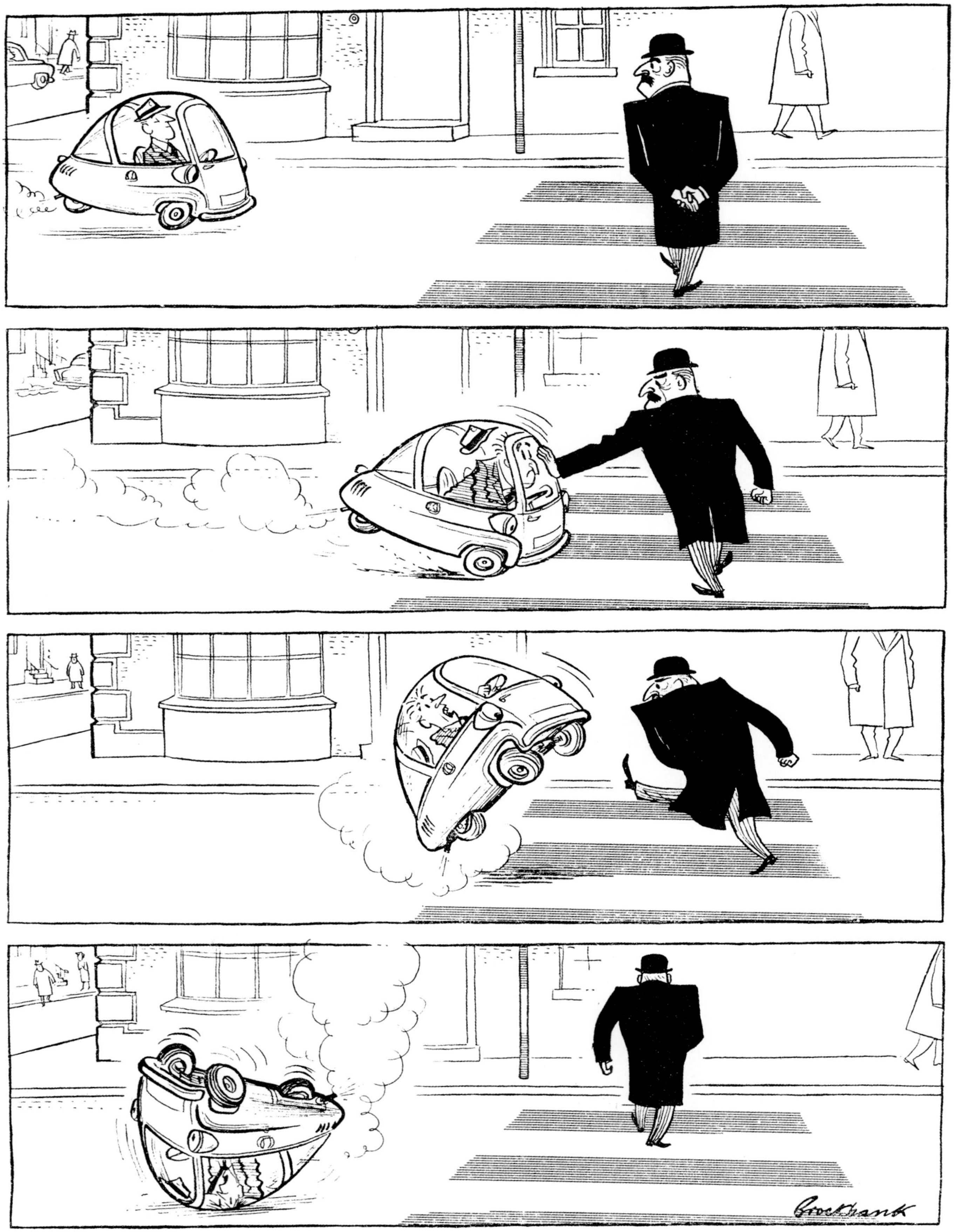
Brockbank

Russell Brockbank, 1957

'*Next: a very easy little question which
I shall put in the form of a few simple
hypothetical syllogisms.*'

John Whitfield Taylor, 1952

'*Never mind me – get cracking on the reviewers.*'

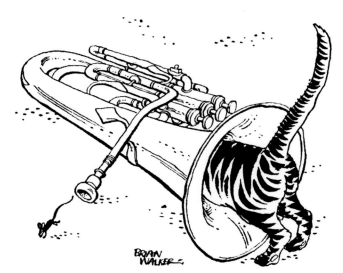

Brian Walker, 1952

- 331 -

Russell Brockbank, 1957

Larry, 1957

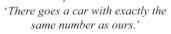

'There goes a car with exactly the
same number as ours.'

Lawrie Siggs, 1952

Gerard Hoffnung, 1957

Norman Thelwell, 1957

George Sprod, 1953

'*Oh, I remember now – it's not the food that's fabulous here; it's the prices.*'

- 333 -

Russell Brockbank, 1953

'*While you're about it, ask him if he knows a good place for lunch.*'

John Whitfield Taylor, 1957

# GERARD HOFFNUNG
## 1925–1959

Hoffnung came to London from Germany as a teenaged refugee in 1939 and by the 1950s he was a British institution. The fertile imagination and sense of the absurd shown in his marvellously quirky caricatures of musicians and their instruments, combined with his own musical skills, led to the celebrated Hoffnung Music Festivals of the late Fifties. His ability to give life to inanimate objects was, according to Hoffnung, beyond his control; 'I would try to draw something, a chair for instance', he wrote, 'and there it would be – with an expression. I had almost nothing to do with it'.

Gerard Hoffnung, 1957

Gerard Hoffnung, 1954

**THE VIOLA**
*(pizzicato)*

Gerard Hoffnung, 1956

Gerard Hoffnung, 1956

Gerard Hoffnung, 1957

THE SOUFFLÉ

1.

2.

Fougasse (Kenneth Bird), 1948

André François, 1957

Anton (Antonia Yeoman), 1953

'*It's supposed to be automatic, but actually you have to press a button.*'

Norman Thelwell, 1957

- 337 -

'*Lot 64. What am I bid?*'

Douglas, 1957

Quentin Blake, 1951

Arnold Frederick Wiles, 1957

'Lately she's been so listless.'

Mervyn Wilson, 1953

'What's happened to the girl who
was here yesterday?'

Henning Gantris, 1953

André François, 1952

Lawrie Siggs, 1957

'*George is waiting for nuclear power.*'

Douglas Lionel Mays, 1953

'*A few more programmes like that and I shall go back to homework.*'

*Motor racing, to the British, seems to be just another spectator sport...*

*...until immediately afterwards, anyway.*

Russell Brockbank, 1953

Keith Waite, 1953

*'Evolution, I suppose you'd call it.'*

Alfred Jackson, 1951

- 341 -

Kenneth Mahood, 1953

*'Poor Henry misses so much, being deaf.'*

Acanthus (Harold Frank Hoar), 1953

'*And this used to be the Torture Chamber.*'

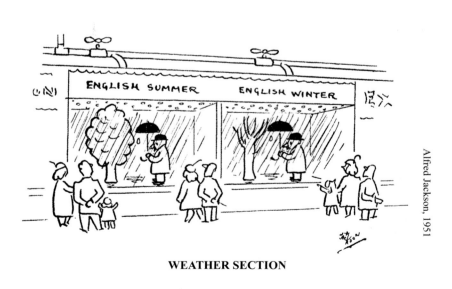

ENGLISH SUMMER  ENGLISH WINTER

**WEATHER SECTION**

Alfred Jackson, 1951

Lawrie Siggs, 1951

'*Does anyone here own car number ZXY 303?*'

George Adamson, 1953

Adamson.

- 343 -

Alberto Fremura, 1959

Frem

William Augustus Sillince, 1954

Sillince

'*You know, children have an instinctive understanding
of the right use of a medium.*'

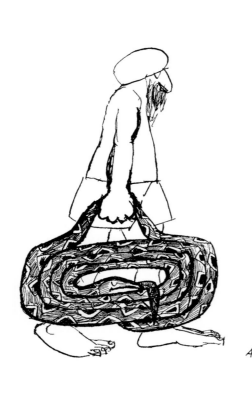

André François, 1956

A.F.

George Sprod, 1953

'I shouldn't eat that sir—it's just possible
that it's part of the ceiling.'

William Scully, 1954

'How much is this one?'

John Whitfield Taylor, 1951

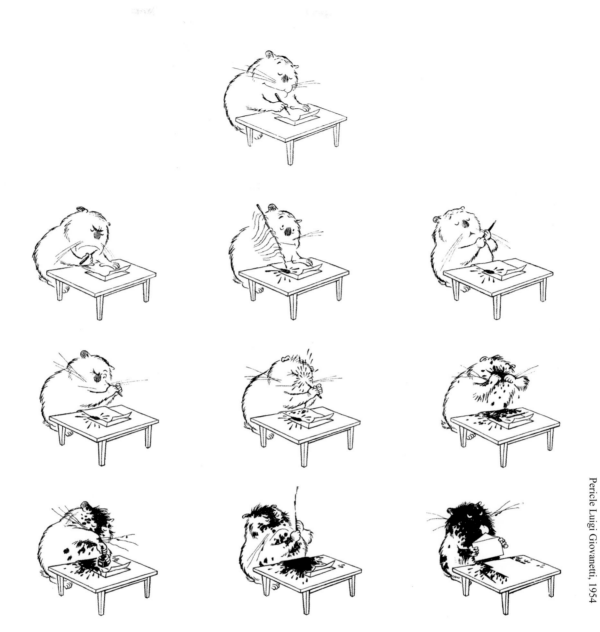

Pericle Luigi Giovanetti, 1954

- 345 -

William Hewison, 1957

*'Electrification,' they says: and gone, gone is the wonder and romance of the Iron Road!'*

*'Are you sure he's finding our way home for us, or does
he think we're still taking him for a walk?'*

*'Are you sure we brought him?'*

George Adamson, 1956

Norman Thelwell, 1956

'They're only breaking these
blasted records so they can do
us out of complimentary meals.'

Russell Brockbank, 1954

Douglas (Douglas England), 1956

William Augustus Sillince, 1959

George Sprod, 1954

'*Last year it was seaweed flies.*'

# How to Kill a Man in Six Efforts BY RONALD SEARLE

1. Love

2. Indifference

3. Jealousy

4. Poison

5. Undernourishment

6. Strength

Ronald Searle, 1954

# ANTON
## ANTONIA YEOMAN

The persona of 'Anton' began as a collaboration between Antonia Yeoman and her brother Harold Underwood Thompson (1911–1996), but as they once wrote: 'please don't ask us how it happens'. During the Second World War Harold was able only to contribute gags, while afterwards, with his advertising career developing, the cartoons became entirely Antonia's in 1949. In the 1960s she dropped 'Anton's' idiosyncratic dark hatching and began using washes, but kept her black humour – and fine eye for dogs and frocks.

- 352 -

Anton (Antonia Yeoman), 1951

*'Do you keep assorted dog biscuits?'*

Anton (Antonia Yeoman), 1961

*'Don't forget that Mr. Stanton helped to make it a pleasant evening too, dear.'*

Anton (Antonia Yeoman), 1942

*'Yes, I admit it is interesting, but please remember WE've been sent out to record the first cuckoo.'*

Anton (Antonia Yeoman), 1944

'Are you together?'

Anton (Antonia Yeoman), 1948

- 353 -

'I must introduce you—you've
got so much in common.'

Anton (Antonia Yeoman), 1947

'Do we wish to let our house, dear?'

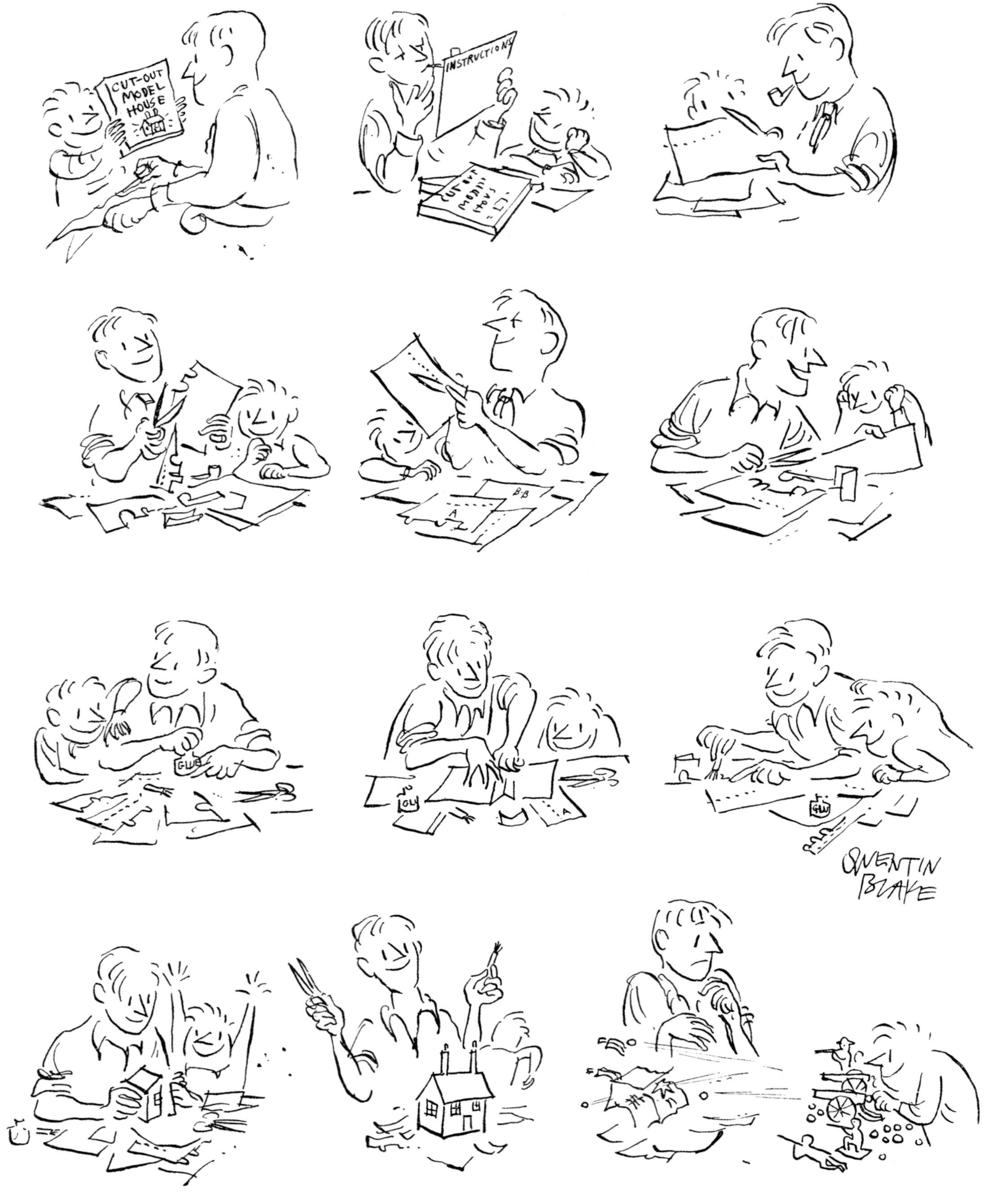
CUT-OUT
MODEL
HOUSE
INSTRUCTIONS
QUENTIN
BLAKE

Quentin Blake, 1954

Giovannetti, 1956

'*Me? Drinking?*'

Lawrie Siggs, 1957

'*Now we'll compare it with his bark and you'll see what I mean.*'

- 355 -

Ronald Searle, 1956

John Whitfield Taylor, 1951

# ·LOOK BEFORE YOU LEAP·

## A CHILD'S GUIDE TO SHOW JUMPING

The opportunity to examine the fences before the start of the competition should never be missed. ⟶

The signal to start is given by a bell, flag or whistle.

A horse or pony is said to have "REFUSED" if he stops in front of a fence... ⟶

.... and to have "FALLEN"... if the shoulders and quarters have touched the ground.

- 356 -

Norman Thelwell, 1956

A competitor is eliminated for showing any fence to a horse after a refusal.

←

Or for unauthorised assistance whether solicited or not.

→

Endless patience is required to reach perfection –

←

But for those who ultimately achieve a clear round - the rewards are many

→

.thelwell.

- 357 -

Norman Thelwell, 1956

Derek Edwards, 1956

Jean-Jacques Sempé, 1959

George Sprod, 1956

'*Well, whatever it is it's bound to be rude.*'

Timothy (Timothy Birdsall), 1959

'*But I always thought you were a Tory.*'

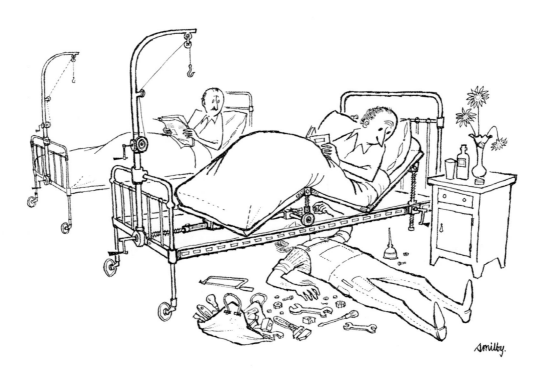

Smilby (Francis Wilford-Smith), 1956

Norman Thelwell, 1956

'Heel!'

Gerard Hoffnung, 1956

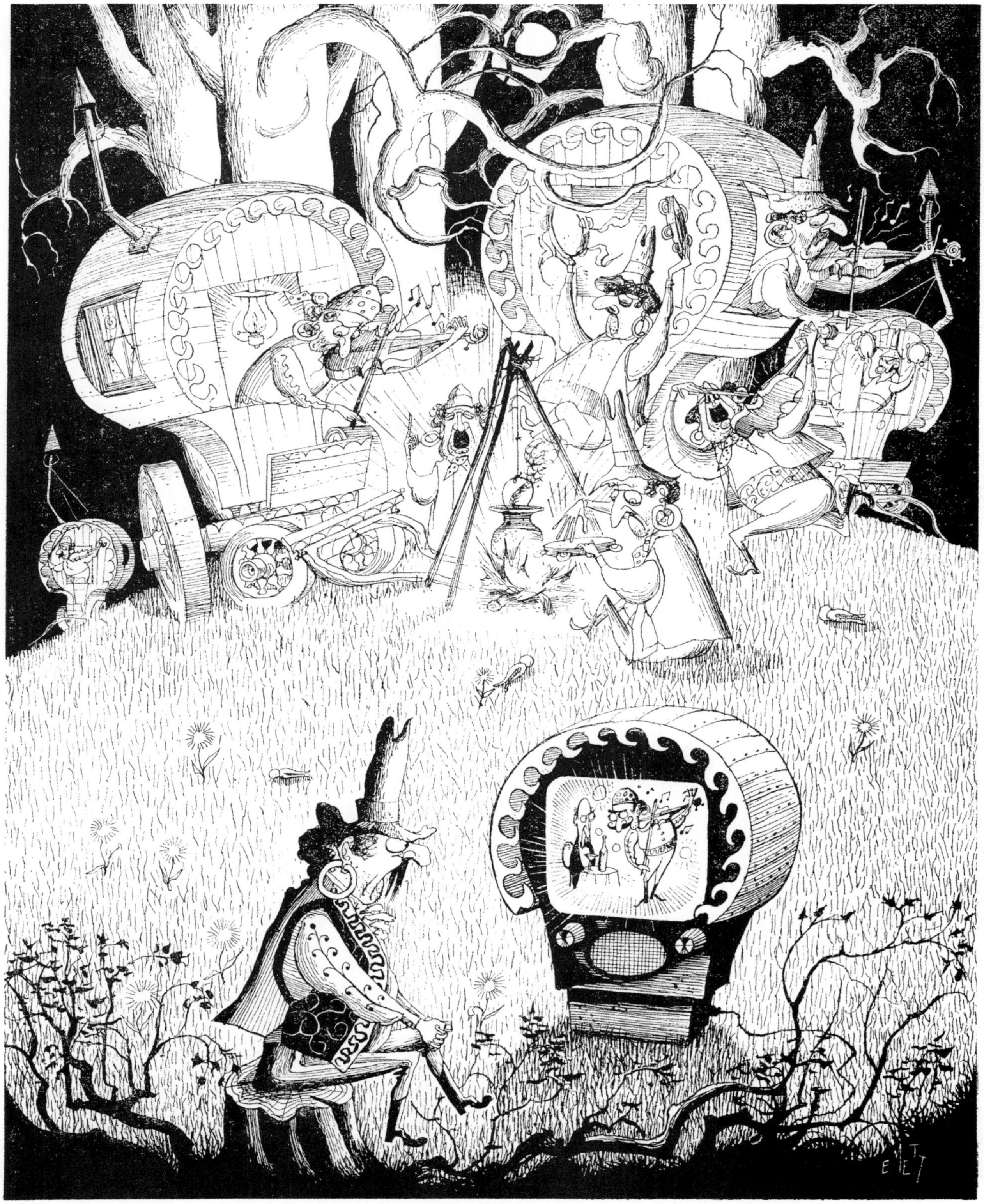

Rowland Emett, 1948

# RONALD SEARLE

## B. 1920

O ne of the world's greatest illustrators, Searle's work for
*Punch* had a tremendous impact. He began contributing on
his return to Britain after spending the Second World War in
the notorious Changi prison camp. Though his bread and butter were
the hundreds of magnificent caricatures he drew for the magazine's
theatre column, Searle produced the brilliant series *The Rake's
Progress*, political cartoons, a clutch of some of *Punch's* best covers,
the spectacular colour inserts *Heroes of Our Time* and a host of full-
page illustrations in his inimitable spiky style.

Ronald Searle, 1957

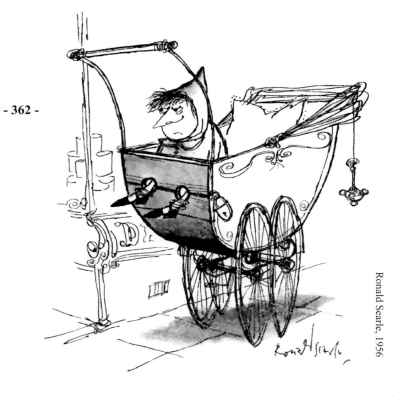

Ronald Searle, 1956

Ronald Searle, 1955

*The Child-hater*

Ronald Searle, 1954

Anton (Antonia Yeoman), 1957

'*Come, Mrs Tankerton – surely that's not all?*'

David Langdon, 1950

'*Oh, for heaven's sake, Granny – you can't expect boxing every night.*'

Russell Brockbank, 1957

Roy Davis, 1957

Alfred Jackson, 1956

John Whitfield Taylor, 1952

Ronald Searle, 1959

*'I hope that child's been innoculated against distemper.'*

George Sprod, 1953

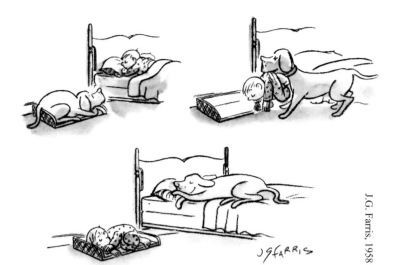

J.G. Farris, 1958

John Whitfield Taylor, 1959

*'En français, Jackson, en français.'*

Rowland Emett, 1953

*"...and then the family portraits in the Long Gallery had to be sold."*

*'Comment – du vin rouge avec le poisson?'*

Walter Goetz, 1957

Quentin Blake, 1957

Anton (Antonia Yeoman), 1951

'I've seen eighteen doctors and seven psychiatrists. It seems I'm suffering from a deep-seated guilt complex about getting things free from the National Health Service.'

Norman Thelwell, 1958

'It's no use making a noise like that! You've been blooded once.'

'*Looking for the main verb, you know.*'

'*But I don't **like** free expression.*'

Ed Fisher, 1959

'There are still a lot of things they haven't worked out.'

David Langdon, 1950

'Now, if all three are there, he's somewhere around the office. If the hat's gone, he's at elevenses; if the hat and umbrella's gone, he's at lunch; if they've all gone, he's left for the day.'

Norman Thelwell, 1959

'Here! Do you want to catch your death of cold?'

Douglas Lionel Mays, 1947

- 372 -

*'Of course, I'm terribly glad I got my degree, mother, but can you honestly see
any man falling in love with a girl who's going to be a nuclear physicist?'*

Jean-Jacques Sempé, 1959

William Augustus Sillince, 1854

'We're rather worried about William.'

# 1960–1979

## Sixties and Seventies

Roy Raymonde, 1961

'Here we go again—conquest—subjection—insurrection—independence...'

Kenneth Mahood, 1960

'I've tried mental cruelty but he seems to like it.'

Bill Tidy, 1960

'Got a record as long as your arm...Escorted off at
White Hart Lane, Molineux, Maine Road, Villa Park...'

*Norman Thelwell, 1962*

*'Money can't buy them happiness.'*

*Alberto Fremura, 1960*

*PAV (Francis Minet), 1960*

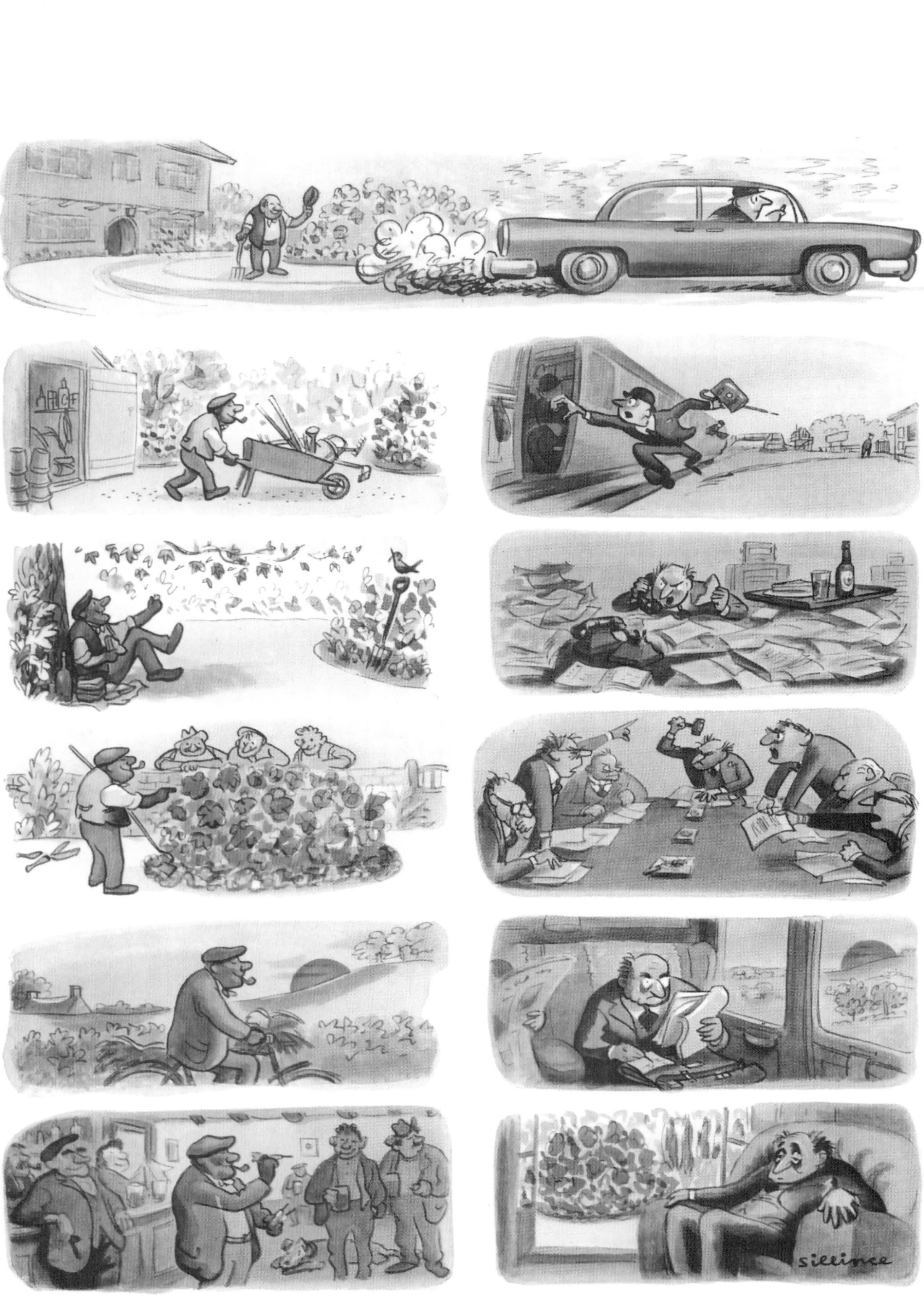
sillince

William Augustus Sillince, 1960

Eric Burgin, 1961

'I've forgotten which tune we're improvising on.'

Don Roberts, 1963

'For God's sake, Gerald, unwind gradually!'

Gahan Wilson, 1960

'Of course if $\int_r^x v^a du = \lim_{n \to \infty} \sum_{i=1}^{n} \left(\frac{i}{n}x\right)^a \cdot \frac{x}{n}$, we're sunk.'

Bud Handelsman, 1969

'I know we've been here for four hundred years, but
we'll certainly pull out as soon as the Britons show
they're able to defend themselves.'

'Actually, I only need one way.'

'Martin still has plenty of virility, although of course
these days most of it goes into real estate.'

Norman Thelwell, 1961

Don Roberts, 1961

Ralph Steadman, 1963

Michael ffolkes (Brian Davis), 1969

*'When we first met he was tremendously rampant.'*

Bill Tidy, 1968

'We'll have to decide! Are we storming the
Winter Palace or the Summer Palace?'

Ed Fisher, 1979

'It's got more special-function keys than you'll
find on many of the larger models: square root,
cosine, logarithmic, integral and exponential
keys. I'd say that more than makes up for the
fact that it doesn't have the number nine!'

Anton 1961

William Augustus Sillince, 1960

'Well, to begin with, it shocks you out of your complacency.'

# OH NO!
# NOT ANOTHER...

**Free Gift**

**Channel**

**Child Star**

**People's Choice**

**Good Cause**

**Great Character**

**Knight**

**Religion**

**Mistake**

Gerald Scarfe, 1962

George Sprod, 1963

'Looks as if the Tate's been
impulse-buying again.'

Bud Handelsman, 1974

'That's my advice as your accountant.
Speaking as your friend, I'd have to
say it was pretty lousy advice.'

Anton (Antonia Yeoman), 1963

'Notice how they all want to play it safe since the Keeler affair?'

John Whitfield Taylor, 1962

'Your supper's in the oven. Walter Gabriel has straightened things out with Ned, but Ena Sharples suspects that Elsie Tanner…'

David McKee, 1964

Michael ffolkes (Brian Davis), 1963

'Very well, Geoffrey – you have received fair warning. I am going to confiscate your brick.'

Hector Breeze, 1963

'The usual mumbo-jumbo about a Pharoah's curse.'

- 384 -

*'You should have consulted the committee before you*
*accepted the Snugfit Truss sponsorship, Major.'*

*'They're getting restless. Okay boys,*
*ham it up—knock the tea-pot over or something.'*

Roy Raymonde, 1962

'Plastics or not—there's always some damned
perfectionist wants the real thing!'

Larry (Terence Parkes), 1962

Albert Edgar Beard, 1963

Michael ffolkes (Brian Davis), 1962

Alexander Steel Graham, 1962

'Isn't that young Miss Taylor who had the
corner table by the Bougainvillaeas?'

'It was such a lovely evening I thought I'd
just toddle down and have my ears syringed.'

Alexander Steel Graham, 1965

'Are you sure it's my turn?...I'm certain I sacked the last one.'

John Whitfield Taylor

'As a first step let us try to get back
to the love-hate relationship.'

Norman Thelwell, 1964

Norman Mansbridge, 1964

Albert Edgar Beard, 1964

'I tell you, Sarge, it's going to be pure hell.'

Quentin Blake, 1964

PAV (Francis Minet), 1965

Lawrie Siggs, 1965

Ray (Raymond Chesterton), 1964

'In this department, sir, the forces for good
exist solely to wipe out evil.'

'You explain it then – all I know is,
they don't spend any time on it!'

Bruce Petty, 1962

'Clay too dry, Miss Melkin—too dry.'

Bud Handelsman, 1978

'Why should you and I bother to come back, Tom? Reincarnation is for people who failed this time around.'

Michael ffolkes (Brian Davis), 1962

'I think I saw an eyelid flicker.'

Tony Holland, 1965

'Then suddenly you wake up and find you're just another thug in a wave of violence.'

William Scully, 1963

*'From here there's a rather fine reflection of St. Paul's.'*

Henning Gantris, 1964

Kenneth Mahood, 1965

*'It's a begging letter.
Boy, have they got the
wrong address.'*

# A Short History of Arms

*In the beginning men quarrelled*

*and, frustrated, resorted to arms*

*Archaic bombardment was devised*

*research and invention provided weapons*

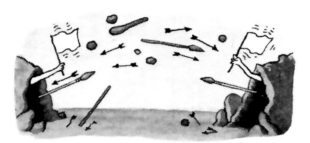

*war became communal—civilians were involved*

*defences were perfected*

*tactics were devised*

*impregnable fortresses were built*

*but always the ultimate weapon was at hand*

*such as gunpowder*

*and war was never the same*

Arnold Roth, 1962

*Classic war became a bore*        *even with the ultimate defence*

*World War I revived the layman's interest with*

*poison gases*        *and weird aerial combat*

*World War II produced nuclear weapons*

*and Peace brought* **ultimate** *nuclear weapons*

*So man resorted to argument, and still more argument, until argument led to . . .*

Arnold Roth, 1962

Tony Holland, 1979

'Fortunately, it says less about me than an
American Express card ever can.'

Edward Frascino, 1966

'Look at him sitting there with the smug self-assurance that the
tide of automation will suddenly ebb at his door.'

Norman Thelwell, 1969

'Turn her round and head for the amusement arcade.'

Leslie Starke, 1971

'I don't believe it's been touched! Where are the reassuring oily finger marks on the steering wheel, the greay smears on the upholstery, the smudges on the paintwork, the footprints on the carpet?'

Bill Tidy, 1968

'...So that's your little game!'

Alexander Steel Graham, 1972

'We were well within the limit on our bathroom scales.'

Anton (Antonia Yeoman), 1963

'Stop laughing, you fool – they're taking the mickey out of people like us.'

# CARICATURES

There were caricatures aplenty in *Punch*'s full-page Big Cuts, usually of the political heavy-hitters of the day. The magazine's tradition of small 'celebrity' caricatures, however, which we showcase here, began perhaps with Linley Sambourne's series of 'Fancy Portraits'. But it was the introduction of film and theatre (and later television) reviews in the twenteith century that opened the magazine's pages week after week to the brilliance of caricatures by stars like Sherriffs, Searle and Hewison. Later in the century Trog (Wally Fawkes) assumed the caricaturing crown.

PUNCH'S FANCY PORTRAITS.—No. 37.

Linley Sambourne, 1881

"O. W."

"O, I feel just as happy as a bright Sunflower!"
*Lays of Christy Minstrelsy.*

Æsthete of Æsthetes!
What 's in a name?
The poet is WILDE,
But his poetry 's tame.

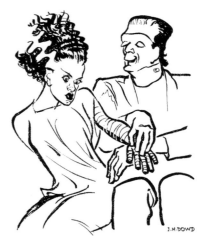

James Henry Dowd, 1935

SYNTHETIC S.A.

The Mate . . . . . ELSA LANCHESTER.
The Monster . . . . KARLOFF.

MR. PUNCH'S FANCY PORTRAITS.

Linley Sambourne, 1889

M. EIFFEL.

"OUR ARTIST'S LATEST TOUR DE FORCE."

Ronald Searle, 1951

[*The Winter's Tale*]

**Jealous King**
*Hermione*—MISS DIANA WYNYARD; *Leontes*—MR. JOHN GIELGUD
*Paulina*—MISS FLORA ROBSON

Ronald Searle, 1961

*[Beyond the Fringe*

PETER COOK
JONATHAN MILLER    DUDLEY MOORE
ALAN BENNETT

Trog (Wally Fawkes), 1984

**BOB DYLAN**

William Hewison, 1960

*Oliver Twist*—KEITH HAMSHERE    *Fagin*—RON MOODY

*[Oliver!*

Robert Stewart Sherriffs, 1957

*[The Monte Carlo Story*

*La Marquise Maria de Crèvecœur*—MARLENE DIETRICH

Robert Stewart Sherriffs, 1957

*[Lust for Life*

*Vincent Van Gogh*—KIRK DOUGLAS

Martin Honeysett, 1971

'It's our biggest seller.'

Tony Holland, 1969

'I couldn't have had a worse start—I came from what's now scheduled as a slum dwelling in a twilight zone of a grey area on the fringe of a development region.'

Larry (Terence Parkes), 1968

Harry Hargreaves, 1965

David Myers, 1977

'Your wife wants to know if you'll
agree to have him put down.'

Mike Williams, 1969

'Strawberry mousse! Strawberry mousse!'

Albert (Albert Rusling), 1969

- 397 -

'I wish we'd got him before rigor mortis set in.'

Chon Day, 1965

'Parties, parties, parties! Why can't we just
stay home and get stoned?'

M. F. Tombs, 1977

Hector Breeze 1965

'That's the universe out there—doesn't it make you feel sort of...arrogant?'

Chic, 1966

Alexander Steel Graham, 1962

'If it's Tim I never want to speak to him
again...If it's Mickey I'm out...If it's Peter I'll
ring him back...If it's Richard I'll take it.'

Larry (Terence Parkes), 1974

Bud Handelsman, 1965

'That slurping sound isn't dubbed in. That's pure Bergman.'

David Langdon, 1965

'Where was it now? Hands Off Cuba, Aldermaston '63,
Clear Out of Vietnam, No Fluoride In Water Supplies…?'

John Whitfield Taylor, 1965

'The natives are restless tonight.'

Kenneth Mahood, 1965

'In this horrible night-mare all the
conventional weapons have been abolished
and we have to fight it out with vomit gas,
itching powder and rubber darts.'

*'I don't know why I don't leave you.'*

*'Oh, I was on tour with this company doing 'Godot'
and we flopped. How about you?'*

*'All this effort, money, sonic bangs - just so a planeload of Commissars
can fly from Moscow to Vladivostock in time for lunch.'*

Michael ffolkes (Brian Davis), 1960

Lawrie Siggs, 1966

*'By the way, thanks for looking after the garden for us
while we were on holiday.'*

Michael Heath, 1967

Cover, 1962

Christopher Reid, 1968

- 402 -

Michael ffolkes (Brian Davis), 1970

'Don't disturb Sir Roger. He's fermenting.'

Bud Handelsman, 1965

'My God, we're missing 'The Great War'!'

Hector Breeze, 1971

'Do you think the directors ever pretend to be us?'

'When we first moved here, it was a charming,
unspoilt little supermarket.'

'The school has a very good record—last year
alone they had seven boys accepted by Oxford,
five by Cambridge and four by Brian Epstein.'

- 403 -

'A combination of various suspicious things. Early morning
tea, then a swim, then bacon and eggs, for lunch fish and
chips, and never asking if there's any mail.'

'My God! Rachel Carson was right.
The hollyhocks are going berserk.'

'Look at it another way—all right,
so you've failed your test, but you've
probably increased your life expectancy.'

RELEGATION
IS
NIGH

'I have absolutely no small talk either.
Shall we smooch?'

- 404 -

'It's agreed then—we cut our ten-minute
tea break down to twenty minutes.'

'You're right!
It is eating ants!'

William Scully, 1969

'Have they developed a strain yet that thrives on neglect?'

Hector Breeze, 1964

'I shan't believe integration's really here
until they let us join the Ku-Klux-Klan.'

Kenneth Mahood, 1965

'We have the ideal marriage—
I love me and he loves him.'

Ken Pyne, 1978

'You mean we all think badminton's a
bloody boring game and we'd all prefer
to spend our evenings in the pub?'

Bruce Petty, 1965

'It won't eat.'

Ed Fisher, 1965

'But it's only what they say—that we
don't breed in captivity.'

Lawrie Siggs, 1966

'Same old story—boy meets girl but doesn't know it.'

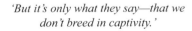

Lawrie Siggs, 1966

'Where you go we go—we're the side effects.'

*Eric Burgin, 1965*

*'Maurice has a wonderful understanding with the children—
they don't try to understand him and he doesn't try to understand them.'*

*Bud Handelsman, 1965*

*'The trustees understand the curriculum requires
you to teach Marxism. We just feel that you're
not making it boring enough.'*

*Hector Breeze, 1969*

*'Are you going to lie there all night wondering whether
there's fluoride in the water?'*

'Oh, it's a two-way street, all right: they give
us Aid, we give them Enlightenment.'

- **408** -

'Well don't just stand there — negotiate!'

'We don't 'fill jobs' here at Consolidated Tank &
Foundry; we offer opportunities for the growth
and enrichment of the individual.'

'Somehow, once you get up the whole day is ruined.'

David Langdon, 1968

'No, I think he's all right to ask the way. It's the chaps in round
black helmets who knock your teeth in.'

Bud Handelsman, 1969

'Oh hell! Are you sure? I was hoping
we were Lust.'

- 409 -

Hector Breeze, 1968

'Let's form a military junta!'

Ed McLachlan, 1966

Clive Collins, 1978

Chon Day, 1963

'I…a woman…answered.
She…a woman…hung up.'

Hector Breeze, 1969

'First of all let's celebrate having come through the
swinging sixties with our prejudices intact.'

Michael Clark, 1972

'They got me on a motoring offence—
I strangled my driving instructor.'

John Whitfield Taylor, 1966

'I've won ten days in Paris with the
companion of my choice.'

Chic (Cyril Alfred Jacob), 1971

'Somehow I don't think we'll ever achieve
a state of equality with Madge Benskin!'

Joseph Mirachi, 1966

'So that's where the spanner went.'

Stan McMurtry, 1967

'Well, gentlemen... Shall we join the ladies?'

Patricia Drennan, 1978

'I have to put up with it in the office,
but I'm damned if I'll be treated
as an equal in my own home!'

Michael ffolkes (Brian Davis), 1968

'The Arts Council keep it just as he left it.'

'Oh God no! Not the '23!'

'You know what I like about you? You don't
talk, talk, talk, talk, talk, talk, talk.'

**- 413 -**

'Obsolescent consumer durables,
obsolescent consumer durables - where's
the good old-fashioned rubbish?'

'Frank is into unofficial strike action... Harry is working to rule...
Bob is into picketing... and Walter here is into impotent rage.'

# NORMAN THELWELL
## 1923-2004

'Thelwell pony' entered the English language after the runaway success of the artist's cartoons for *Punch* recording the exploits of small girls and their stout (and disobedient) ponies. An outstanding artist, Thelwell contributed over 1,500 cartoons to the magazine. Though best-known as a brilliant recorder of the countryside scene, Thelwell's range was far broader. While he claimed to have 'no axes to grind and no torches to bear', his sensitive cartoons on race and immigration and more passionate responses to the increasing degradation of the environment show this was not entirely true.

Norman Thelwell, 1955

Norman Thelwell, 1969

*'He's asked for political asylum.'*

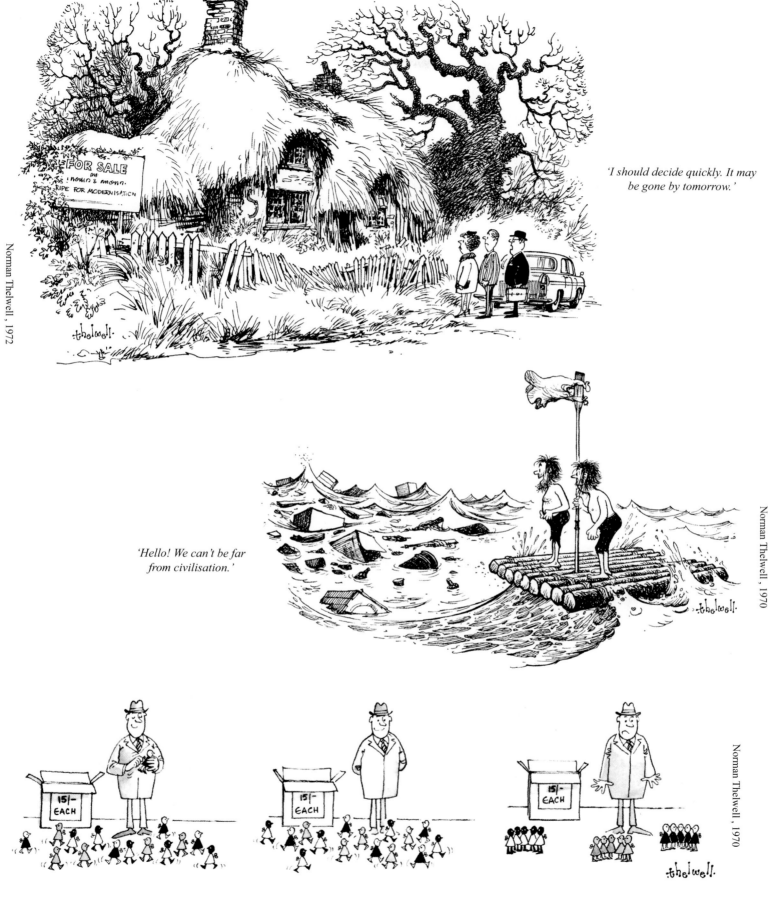

'I should decide quickly. It may be gone by tomorrow.'

Norman Thelwell, 1972

- 415 -

'Hello! We can't be far from civilisation.'

Norman Thelwell, 1970

Norman Thelwell, 1970

Michael Heath, 1968

'You've overdone the aftershave again.'

William Scully, 1968

'It may be the age of the Bomb, nuclear power and
inter-continental missiles, but, thank heaven, it's
also the age of non-drip paint.'

Charles Saxon, 1968

'Linda and I are getting a divorce, and we
divided up our friends. I got you.'

Tony Holland, 1969

'If there were a political opinion poll tomorrow,
which party would you say you'd vote for?'

Michael ffolkes (Brian Davis), 1978

'That's the deal then. We give you our gold and you give us
something called a Spanish omelette.'

Norman Thelwell, 1967

'I shouldn't paddle. They might not let you back.'

Bill Tidy, 1968

'Yes, but is there any news of the iceberg.'

Arnold Frederick Wiles, 1969

- 418 -

Roy Nixon, 1969

Hector Breeze, 1978

'It's the same year after year–nobody ever turns up!'

Larry (Terence Parks), 1969

Martin Honeysett, 1977

'I have your file with me right
now, Mr. Brown, and I'm rushing
through things as fast as I can.'

Mike Williams, 1977

'We'd like to appeal against the light.'

Ed McLachlan, 1969

'We have reason to believe you are carrying
certain substances of a hallucinogenic nature.'

Michael ffolkes (Brian Davis), 1979

'We've decided against divorce. Neither of us
wants custody of the dog.'

Leslie Starke, 1969

'Oh, all right then—take down the notices.
Bring back the ash-trays.'

John Whitfield Taylor, 1968

'I thought you knew I'm on a research fellowship.'

Quentin Blake, 1973

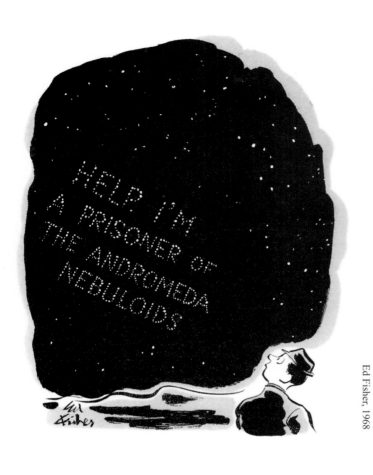

Ed Fisher, 1968

Ken Pyne, 1978

'My father wanted me to go into his
insurance business and I wanted to go
into the theatre, so we compromised.'

Arnold Frederick Wiles, 1975

'My agent said it was a remake of the 'Prisoner of Zenda'
but apparently it's a commercial for Rawlplugs.'

Norman Thelwell, 1969

'We've got another leak.'

Posy Simmonds, 1972

Chic (Cyril Alfred Jacob), 1970

'Damn! Somebody's pinched our spot!'

Martin Honeysett, 1978

Bill Tidy, 1970

'Aw c'mon, Genghis – we need one more to
make up a horde!'

'I understand you've
sacked your gardener.'

Albert (Albert Rusling), 1970

David Myers, 1978

'We lost all our snaps but we knew you'd like
to see how we looked on holiday.'

Michael Heath, 1969

'We'll still see each other. It's just that as
a group we feel washed up.'

Ed Fisher, 1964

'Dad, can I join the Jehovah's Witnesses?'

Bud Handelsman, 1971

'I'm afraid I can't help you; civil liberties are outside
my domain. I specialise in jungle law.'

Roy Raymonde, 1971

'Come, come, Mr. D'Arcy – I told you it
was going to be a big job.'

Martin Honeysett, 1970

'I will be brief.'

Hector Breeze, 1972

'The arrangement's over, Cyril—
you'll have to choose between us.'

Mike Williams, 1971

'Actually Bernard likes to walk. It's the dog that needs a pint.'

Ed McLachlan, 1975

'Well, here we are, Maudsley—we're in big cat country at last!'

Kenneth Mahood, 1970

Stan McMurtry, 1967

'I just shook his hand and he was sick.'

Mike Williams, 1978

Michael ffolkes (Brian Davis), 1973

'I must say, Mr Baskerville, we had expected something larger.'

Ray Lowry, 1979

'We've cut out the middle-men altogether. Instead of
booking a band we just let the kids and the bouncers
kick the hell out of each other all night!'

Merrily Harpur, 1978

'Yes, I do consider myself intelligent.
I only worry about cellulite if there's
nothing special on the News.'

Kenneth Mahood, 1973

'I must say I'm enjoying my metamorphosis from
dirty old man to avant garde eroticist!'

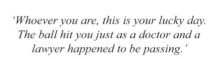

Bud Handelsman, 1978

'Whoever you are, this is your lucky day.
The ball hit you just as a doctor and a
lawyer happened to be passing.'

Pete Williams, 1973

'Sandy Gall…News at Ten…Canta Pero…'

'Sisters, let's leave the men
to their mindless chatter
and get the cigars.'

Michael Heath, 1977

'I don't know why they resent
us so much—we only take the
jobs they don't want...doctors,
scientists, engineers...'

Ed McLachlan, 1979

**HER MASTER'S VOICE**

'The 4.30 a.m. time check is brought to you
by the spirit of mounting personal problems,
anxieties and hostile vibes.'

'I'd better warn the passengers,
Chief. We seem to have inadvertently
violated Hugh Hefner's air space.'

'I hate to do this, but I've just taken
on a huge mortgage.'

'Why can't I get married in the firm's time?
I got pregnant in the firm's time.'

'Since you ask, I had you, Samantha, because
the birthrate was falling; and you, David, as
revenge on society; and you, Mark, as a bid
for lost youth; and you, Jason, were a mistake.'

'I'll answer your questions if you'll take this
supermarket trolley back for me.'

'Yes?'

# THE SPACE RACE

The Cold War rivalry between America and the Soviet Union for dominance in outer space gripped the world for two decades. *Punch* recorded the successes and tensions of the Space Race from the launch of Sputnik – the start of the titanic contest – to the safe return of orbiting space mutts Belka and Strelka (accompanied by a grey rabbit, 42 mice, 2 rats, and a number of flies), Neil Armstrong's moon walk of 1969 and the technological spin-offs that found their way into our kitchens – and possibly vice versa.

George Sprod, 1960

*'The food wasn't bad really. We had that concentrated stuff, and there were a lot of rats and mice and plants and things for extras.'*

Kenneth Mahood, 1970

*'Frankly comrade, I don't think bringing back the heel of a space boot and what looks like the remains of Armstrong's lunch is a great step forward for Soviet science.'*

Leslie Starke, 1965

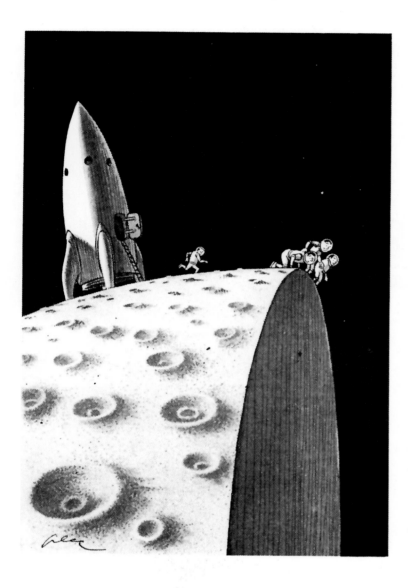

'We're one up on the Russkis.
An electric razor is now standard equipment.'

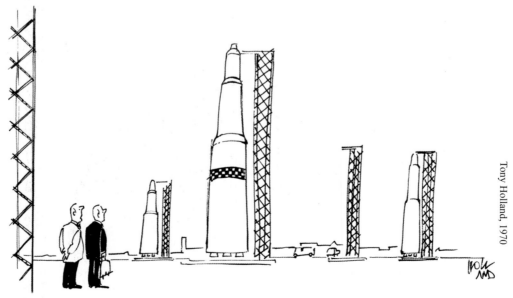

'Actually, they're spin-offs from a project to produce
heat-resistant kitchenware.'

Leslie Starke, 1974

'Your car will be ready in a couple of weeks, sir. Our senior partner is personally handling the final series of road tests.'

Michael Heath, 1978

'He sold out years ago.'

Martin Honeysett, 1974

'As far as I'm concerned he could stay out all night.'

Stan McMurtry, 1968

'Mr Pickard! I asked you not to get him too excited!'

Bud Handelsman, 1973

'Or, if you don't mind about the ruins not being very old,
I can put you on a flight to Belfast.'

John Whitfield Taylor, 1968

'Oh, God – not another moral victory.'

Bernard Cookson, 1974

'I began by going back to nature and
ended up by going to seed.'

David Myers, 1971

'Skimped a bit on the lifeboats, haven't they.'

David Hawker, 1975

'We went round the world last year but didn't like it.'

- 436 -

Michael Heath, 1970

'Remember me, we used to play in the 'Syncopated Washboard Band' back in 1956?'

Bud Handelsman, 1976

'Our token Black—is that really how you think of
yourself, Ms Corwin? You're much more than that,
I assure you. You're also our token woman.'

Mike Williams, 1975

'For God's sake control yourself, Mason—
he's not a real shop steward!'

- 437 -

Martin Honeysett, 1976

'He didn't want anything elaborate.'

'Has this film been heavily cut, or is
copulation really that jerky?'

Merrily Harpur, 1978

Ray Lowry, 1976

'For God's sake hurry, woman. Monsieur Monet's fallen in the lily pond again!'

Ionicus (Joshua Charles Armitage), 1974

'Every week I tell him we don't sell the Church Times or the Methodist Recorder...'

David Myers, 1977

Bud Handelsman, 1975

'No, no, you're not disturbing us. We were
just horsing around listening to Webern,
discussing Wittgenstein, and stuff like that.'

Hector Breeze, 1978

'Could I take a message or anything?
They all seem to be at lunch.'

David Langdon, 1966

'Sorry, chaps. The Russians want to see a typical
British bus with a typical British bus crew.'

Nick (Nicholas Hobart), 1979

Martin Honeysett, 1976

*'Now clear off outside and play.'*

Michael ffolkes (Brian Davis), 1976

*'Seven Deadly Sins are enough. We're dumping Incompetence.'*

Ed McLachlan, 1976

*'You urgently need a holiday, Mr Abthorpe—
might I suggest Lourdes?'*

Norman Thelwell, 1960

David Langdon, 1976

*'He wants twenty-five per cent of the gross, with an agreed minimum
advance guarantee, plus doing our own tidying up.'*

Albert (Albert Rusling), 1977

'I could only afford the one week.'

William Scully, 1976

'Good grief! this balance-sheet won't do – why damn it,
a child could understand it.'

Bruce Petty, 1964

L Spencer, 1976

'You don't often see a real
silk lining, these days...'

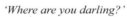

'Where are you darling?'

Michael Heath, 1978

Sally Artz, 1977

'One by one, they all grew up... left home... married...
divorced... came drifting back.'

David Myers, 1977

'Hear the chain squeaking? – I tell you he's on a bike.'

Ross (Harry Ross Thomson), 1968

'He's terribly shy. It was his turn
to take off his shirt.'

Ken Pyne, 1977

'The trouble these day is that the jet-set
is full of the people that I originally
joined the jet-set to get away from.'

Michael ffolkes (Brian Davis), 1977

'What do you mean, no?'

Martin Honeysett, 1975

Kenneth Mahood, 1977

'I'll have a large portion of whatever
the EEC has a mountain of.'

- 445 -

David Myers, 1977

'It's tight across the shoulders when I do this.'

Ray Lowry, 1977

'It's been a truly harrowing experience. It was almost impossible
to combine the right degree of reverence with my nauseating
stream of trivial, mindless chit-chat.'

David Langdon 1978

'Always a bit of an anti-climax—having to queue
up in the rain for a No. 76 to Ponders End.'

Hector Breeze, 1978

'Do you realise that if we lived in Epping we'd
boast about having been here?'

'I don't care if all the other
boys do it—you're not
using my eye make up.'

Michael Heath, 1973

Ross (Harry Ross Thomson), 1978

'Have you noticed how up-to-date the
nostalgia's beginning to look?'

Ray Lowry, 1975

'Unfortunately there's no way of knowing
whether this is a gang of Teds about to leap on
us and kick our teeth in, or a gang of poseurs
hanging about waiting for the next trend.'

William Scully, 1978

'Why, Kilburn, how quaint! You want a rise
because you deserve one.'

Bud Handelsman, 1976

'The authorities have denied permission to film the actual
street fighting. I have, however, obtained clearance to
show you my room at the Hilton, and here it is.'

Ed McLachlan, 1976

- 448 -

Merrily Harpur, 1979

'I want something completely expressionless.'

William Scully, 1978

'But darling, we have a nice house in a nice locality, a smart car, central heating, take our holidays abroad. Haven't we grown out of the Labour Party?'

Ken Pyne, 1979

'For heaven's sake, Brian! Can't you forget for one minute that you're a chartered surveyor.'

RODIN'S
HOT
BATH - WATER

Larry (Terence Parkes), 1979

Noel Ford, 1979

'Worked out rather well on the whole… chap next door
wanted a Steinway and I wanted a bar.'

# MAXIHEATH

*"OK, You can come out now—
the fuzz have gone."*

*"Blast! My stocking's just gone."*

*"You've got the most beautiful nose."*

Michael Heath, 1969

Martin Honeysett, 1979

'Strange, you don't usually see gulls this far inland.'

Stan McMurtry, 1978

Mike Williams, 1974

'A pfennig for your thoughts, Hieronymus.'

Harley L Schwadron, 1979

*'Good morning, Miss Lazarus. Give me your tired, your poor, your huddled masses yearning to breathe free, the wretched refuse of your teeming shore, send these, the homeless, tempest tossed, to me.'*

Michael Heath, 1979

*'I can't get '79 at all—are we still going to discos? What should we be wearing? Are we sniffing or drinking...?'*

Ray Lowry, 1975

*'We feel that this country needs and wants a revival of the same spirit which helped and sustained us in the darkest hours of our island's history ... I refer, of course, to Beatlemania.'*

# 1980–1992
## The Eighties and Beyond

Albert (Albert Rusling), 1980

*'Cocktail parties, cocktail parties.'*

Larry (Terence Parkes), 1980

John Whitfield Taylor, 1983

*'Deborah! I thought you were supposed to be at Greenham Common.'*

*'I think it's time we took the decorations down.'*

Martin Honeysett, 1981

*'We have got your gnome and unless you trim your side of the hedge by Sunday...'*

Stan McMurtry, 1980

*'Squatters!'*

David Myers, 1980

*'At home is one thing. At the office you must snap out of defeats without feeling shattered.'*

William Scully, 1980

'We're celebrating. It's twenty years to the day since
Harry first began prostituting his art.'

Sally Artz, 1980

Michael Heath, 1981

'I'm afraid I must replace you, Miss Thomas—
you are releasing in me frustrations and passions
which I normally reserve for the business.'

Hector Breeze, 1980

'Right, that's Stage One of my plan to dominate
the world successfully accomplished!'

'I'd say loosen his flies but who listens to sex therapists?'

Arnold Frederick Wiles, 1982

'I drink to pluck up the courage to order
ridiculous sounding cocktails.'

Merrily Harpur, 1980

- 457 -

'So I gave it to him straight, I did—'In a time of
recession, go for expansion, borrow, re-equip
and fight back,' I said...'

Alan de la Nougerede, 1980

'There's only one thing to know about being a
dormouse. Everything eats a dormouse.'

Michael ffolkes (Brian Davis), 1980

'Professor Ziegler's working on a way
to get our research grant renewed.'

'We get up at six o'clock every morning to milk
the EEC agricultural subsidies.'

'It's such a nice day we've decided to stay on the beach.'

'He recoiled at something I said, Dr Momfret,
and refuses to come out.'

- 459 -

'My God, they've become piper resistant!'

'Well, so much for Plan 'A'.'

Michael Heath, 1980

Stan McMurtry, 1980

'Well, Mr Scroggins, you've heard what the Inspector's slipping me for a conviction—can you top that?'

John Whitfield-Taylor, 1983

'When you say you have a terminal malfunction, Jackson, I trust you are speaking of yourself and not that five thousand pounds' worth of new hardware in the office.'

David Haldane, 1980

'My one ambition is to evolve into something that's capable of making the occasional witty remark?'

Ken Pyne, 1980

'I went on an ego trip once and nobody noticed.'

'*Will you be paying by cheque, credit card, money, or are you shoplifting?*'

'*To the good old days when you could just come right out with it and offend whoever you pleased and nobody cared!*'

'*Shall we carry on with our idyllic existence or shall we break for coffee?*'

'*Dashed funny how insignificant Australia becomes when there isn't a Test against them!*'

'It's an old Japanese recipe.'

'Well, dialect jokes, mainly—corgis, alsatians, beagles...'

'We used to keep piranha fish.'

'Look, I'm sorry you're so depressed, dear, but I've
told you before never to ring me at the office!'

'...Delayed by subsidence of the line at Didcot, caused
by heavy pressures on clay deposits laid down in the
Jurassic period and perhaps later calcium deposits...'

'It's clear from reading your report, Anderson,
that you have emerged unscathed from the
information explosion.'

Quentin Blake, 1981

David Haldane, 1980

'Listen! There it is again – that persistent, dull knocking sound.'

Hector Breeze, 1981

'Let's dispense with the formalities, shall we?
We're all on first-name terms here!'

Merrily Harpur, 1980

'Yes, darling! Mummy has to keep her hands lovely in
case she ever wants to go back to brain surgery.'

Banx (Jeremy Banks), 1981

BANX

'Well, what kind of curse did you expect? He was nine.'

Noel Ford, 1981

'If it please, M'Lud, the witness prefers to cross his heart, turn around and spit three times.'

SAY IT WITH FLOWERS

THIS IS A STICK UP

Stan McMurtry, 1981

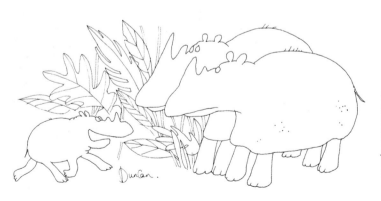

Riana Duncan, 1981

'We made it! We made it! We're on the Endangered Species list!'

'Uh—uh! Her attention's wandered—
this is costing precious points.'

Bill Stott, 1981

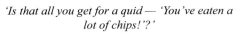

Bill Tidy, 1981

'Is that all you get for a quid — 'You've eaten a
lot of chips!'?'

Ken Pyne, 1980

Hector Breeze, 1980

'Actually, I collapsed while taking part in the East
Grimpton Operatic Society's production of Faust.'

Alan de la Nougerede, 1980

'I'm not asking you to serve me – just to include
me in your conversation.'

Ed McLachlan, 1980

'You say there are some university students waiting for me?'

Bud Handelsman, 1981

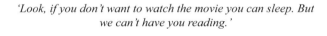

'Look, if you don't want to watch the movie you can sleep. But
we can't have you reading.'

Stan McMurtry, 1980

'I think I'm getting a chemistry set.'

Michael ffolkes (Brian Davis), 1980

'If we get planning permission, we'll call it Venice.'

Peter Birkett, 1981

'Well, this certainly buggers our plan to conquer the Universe.'

- 469 -

Geoffrey Dickinson, 1980

'Well — bang goes the first of my
New Year resolutions.'

Sidney Harris, 1981

'Pleasant surroundings, excellent food, good conversation...
and yet I'm not completely comfortable.'

Banx (Jeremy Banks), 1981

'Looks like the research boys really came up with something this time.'

Ed McLachlan, 1981

'My God! Gramophone sniffing!'

David Hawker, 1981

'Actually, that's the beauty of a placebo.
It just gives the illusion of an overdose.'

Albert (Albert Rusling), 1980

'Car keys!'

Michael Heath, 1981

*'It's what he asked for.'*

Alan de la Nougerede, 1981

*'They want to negotiate a musical instruments limitation treaty.'*

SINGLES
NIGHT
8 till 2

Simon Bond, 1981

David Hawker, 1981

'I do hope this is undiscovered and not passé.'

Peter Birkett, 1981

'I'm getting bored—let's go and bully Molesworth again.'

Michael Heath, 1981

'I can't stand him, really, but I quite like dressing him up.'

Nick (Nicholas Hobart), 1981

'Serves her right. She was always whining about women
not being allowed to participate in the services.'

Ken Pyne, 1981

'This is Shangri-la?'

Merrily Harpur, 1981

'Your accountant will have explained the difference between tax evasion and tax avoidance – well, the same principle applies to birth control.'

Albert (Albert Rusling), 1981

'How long are you going to be in there?'

# MICHAEL FFOLKES
## BRIAN DAVIS
## 1925-1988

**M**ichael ffolkes claimed to have introduced women with sex appeal to the pages of *Punch*. A larger-than-life character whose pen name was assumed after leafing through *Burke's Peerage*, ffolkes' voluptuous ladies were just one of the broad cast of characters who inhabited his cartoons. Ancient Egypt, mythology and decadent aristos were favourite subjects, but he could turn out gags on the mating rituals of peacocks and planning permission in Venice. Ffolkes frequently used washes, overlaid with his characteristic delicate scribbly penwork.

- 474 -

Michael ffolkes, 1982

'He used to be Lust. Now he calls himself Nostalgia.'

Michael ffolkes, 1968

'Fortunately for him he has the best left hook in the school.'

Michael ffolkes, 1986

'I wouldn't say you were a wrong number. We haven't met yet.'

Michael ffolkes, 1969

'I like this one. It's simple.'

Michael ffolkes, 1977

'The one in the grey suit is the author. The others are accountants.'

Michael ffolkes, 1972

'My God, McGregor, what do you mean – it's only a game?'

Michael ffolkes, 1972

'Sometimes I wish I hadn't burned mine.'

Michael Heath, 1981

'Well, if Teddy refuses to pay
alimony to Sindy, you must
get a court order.'

Mike Williams, 1981

'I made it! I made it! I'm into the quarter-finals!'

Henry Martin, 1981

'Behind the plotting and scheming in every office,
there is someone doing the actual work and that
someone, Rogers, better be you.'

Nick (Nicholas Hobart), 1981

'Thank God, their morale remained high
right up to the end.'

Merrily Harpur, 1982

'They spend three years in the Atlantic and
then run up the rivers to spawn.'

Martin Honeysett, 1982

'Head Office have promised us a closed circuit television by next year.'

Roy Raymonde, 1982

'We never could see eye to eye on the subject of decadence, could we, Jocelyn?'

Ed Fisher, 1982

'My God, is every fin-de-siècle like this?'

Noel Ford, 1981

'Here they come again—doesn't the National Trust ever give up?'

Ed McLachlan, 1981

'Here's the bastard now and he's carrying our Maude's bladder.'

'It doesn't matter. Nothing I say matters.'

'How can we get it out, without ruining his suit?'

'He's my social worker.'

Merrily Harpur, 1982

'Country women are so intrepid—there's nothing too
horrible for them to make into a delicious paté.'

Noel Ford, 1982

'We're going to have to split those two up.'

John Donegan, 1982

'Miss Nugent! The Christmas party was over months ago.'

Peter Birkett, 1982

'It was my poor sense of direction that robbed me
of a literary career – I never could discover where
the hell Bloomsbury was.'

Bill Stott, 1981

'I think I understand Wayne's drawing difficulties now, Mr Bradshaw...'

Stan McMurtry, 1981

EXPRESS
BINGO
WIN
THOUSANDS!

END OF WORLD
— OFFICIAL!

Michael Heath, 1981

'It's only my father, he'll be gone in a minute.'

# Harpur The NIGHTMARES of DREAM TOPPING

An everyday story of weekend folk

THE NIGHTMARES ARE DOWN IN THE VILLAGE BUYING PIRITON WHEN THEY SEE AN OLD FORGE....

Look! A blacksmith, children! You're very lucky to see one! "A mighty man is he with large and sinewy hands, and the muscles of his brawny arms are strong as IRON BANDS!"

A dying craft! We moved here just in time!

How do you know so much about them? Did they have them in Hampstead when you were a boy?

No, but many's the time, coming home from school, I used to recite Longfellow...

THEY GO IN TO WATCH THE SPARKS FLY LIKE CHAFF.

Do you forge your own iron bands?

No, it's the customers who wear the iron bands these days, thanks to the punk movement. Of course, I also do exotic iron underwear, mail order, naturally....

I suppose the cost of postage is not the least macabre aspect of it.....

Exactly. In fact ladies often call in person for a spot of spot welding...

These bellows suddenly seem Freudian...

Right! You kids had better go. This is no place for children...

No! Let the little ones stay! This is a family forge — I also do doner kebabs.

Well, shame to let a good furnace go to waste. Chili sauce?

Janet Reger should have sold these in HER underwear shops....she might not have gone bust!

Bust is as bust does

This is a truly memorable kebab..... I'm going to write a poem about it...

NEXT WEEK: A SORE TRIAL.

Merrily Harpur, 1983

Martin Honeysett, 1981

'Just because it's in his own hand, Mrs Figmarsh, doesn't automatically make it a legal will.'

Noel Ford, 1982

'Naturally, when I volunteered to become a
guinea-pig, it never occured to me ...'

Peter Birkett, 1982

'I think I preferred it when he just did voices.'

Michael Heath, 1982

'Don't take any notice of them – they're doing a series for the BBC.'

I MAY NOT KNOW MUCH ABOUT ART BUT I KNOW WHERE THE GENTS IS

Larry (Terence Parkes), 1983

Merrily Harpur, 1982

'I suppose it's the element of danger, but it's the cigarette
afterwards that's really terrific!'

John Donegan, 1982

'We had one or two power cuts while you were away,
Gerald. I'm afraid you were one of them.'

David Haldane, 1982

'Don't you think we should at least try to talk him out of it?'

Ian Jackson, 1984

'Well, well, if it isn't the early bird!'

**- 485 -**

Christof (Christof Eugster), 1987

Banx (Jeremy Banks), 1982

'You're being reincarnated as a mayfly, Mr Hoskins – have a nice day.'

Banx (Jeremy Banks), 1982

'Put it this way, we could try to breed—or I could eat you.'

Bill Tidy, 1981

'No, sir, the Chief Constable lost a ball yesterday.'

Bud Handelsman, 1982

'Sexual harassment? Because I admired your notebook?'

Noel Ford, 1981

'I see you finally had a word with Jenkins about his untidy mowing.'

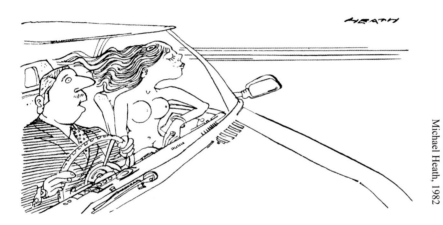

Michael Heath, 1982

'I don't normally give lifts.'

Nick (Nicholas Hobart), 1982

'OK, everyone's gone – you can pick it up now.'

Peter Birkett, 1982

'Honest to God, Lord Lucan – none of us squealed!'

Robert Thompson, 1991

'We'll put it on at £95,000 and hope the athlete's foot doesn't show on the survey.'

Bernard Cookson, 1982

'Look, if it upsets you so much, Harry...'

Holte (Trevor Holder), 1982

'According to the very small print at the bottom of your late husband's policy, everything goes to the printers.'

Martin Ross, 1991

'Foot off the clutch, gently.'

'Bloody hell, Jeanette, I thought you'd cancelled the Jehovah's Witnesses.'

Banx (Jeremy Banks), 1982

P J Rigby, 1982

'Suddenly Fiona screamed at him like a scalded cat.'

- 489 -

'Oh no, it's coming up to the mating season again.'

Tony Husband, 1991

Neil Bennett, 1992

'You see? He's a different dog when he smiles.'

John Donegan, 1982

John Donegan, 1982

*'You again, Mr Philbean? Dear me, dear me, don't
you ever get away with anything?'*

Merrily Harpur, 1982

*'As soon as my nail varnish
is dry I'm going to claw my
way to the top.'*

Banx (Jeremy Banks), 1983

*'It's all right, Sophie, here come ours now.'*

Ray Lowry, 1983

'No, I'm sorry—if I let you keep your underpants on, I'd have
to let everyone keep their underpants on.'

'Are you sure you've been house-hunting
before, Tel?'

'Open up, Benny—Fraud Squad.'

'This is the voice of Moderation. I wouldn't go so far
as to say we have actually seized the radio station.'

# MIND DOCTORS

Always at the mercy of their subconscious, the mind doctors fascinated *Punch*'s cartoonists as far back as the 1930s. Psychiatrists, psychoanalysts, psychologists, shrinks – and their clients, on the couch and off – were to be a continuing source of inspiration for decades to come.

Tony Husband, 1988

*'The commuters are here.'*

William Augustus Sillince, 1938

*'My dear - he simply twisted my subconscious round his little finger.'*

Anton (Antonia Yeoman), 1952

*'Tell me more about this kleptomaniac tendency, Mrs Henderson.'*

'There's nothing I can do for you–you ARE a duck.'

Noel Ford, 1984

'It all stems from the time I discovered that the Consumers'
Association despises everything I possess.'

William Scully, 1965

Harley Schwadron, 1986

'You're right, Doc, it is a miracle cure. I'll have another.'

Micheal Heath, 1969

'Basically you're not bad, it's just that everybody
expects you to be bad, and that makes you bad.'

Leo Cullum, 1982

Holte (Trevor Holder), 1985

'. . . Thought we'd have a nice pot of tea, for a change.'

Mike Williams, 1982

'Smokies!'.

Clive Collins, 1982

Alan de la Nougerede, 1982

'I understand he makes a fantastic living
lecturing on his technique.'

Ed Fisher, 1982

'Actually, I'm no longer a drone.
I'm a pollen consultant.'

Matt (Matthew Pritchett), 1988

'Would you mind if you passively smoked?'

David Haldane, 1982

'OK, I'll nip round the back and create a diversion.'

John Whitfield Taylor, 1982

'We like the plot, Miss Austen, but all this
effing and blinding will have to go.'

...PLEASE WELCOME
DARRIL C. WADE, JR.
AUTHOR OF THE CURRENT
BEST SELLER
"ALONE AGAINST THE SEA"
SOON TO BE A MAJOR
MOTION PICTURE.

Henry Martin, 1982

Nick (Nicholas Hobart), 1982

'Sid, this place may not be as
tough as we thought.'

David Myers, 1982

'I must say, this one's as bright as a button.'

Martin Honeysett, 1982

Stan McMurtry, 1982

'Why can't we have what we had last year — leg?'

Bud Grace, 1983

'*Bombay! Now there's a crazy town. I had dinner with a lady snake charmer. I don't know if she was out to get me, but this morning I woke up with a mongoose in my dhoti. And talk about your untouchables, you ought to see my wife. But, seriously, folks...*'

Banx (Jeremy Banks), 1982

'*Personally, I preferred him the way he was before the exorcism.*'

Michael Heath, 1980

'*'Ere, look—you can stick things with it!*'

Mike Williams, 1983

'*We're out of paper.*'

'No, mate—this is Purgatory. That's Eternity over there.'

'Here's my card. It has an area that you can scratch 'n' sniff.'

'Forget the Beverley Hills Diet. Don't even think about the
Scarsdale method. Stick with the F-Plan high-fibre, and
drink lots of orange juice.'

'What would you like to do?—You can either come
with me and Nanny to the South of France or you can
go and stay with your mother at Greenham Common.'

John Donegan, 1983

*'The usual? I serve six hundred drinks a day and
I'm supposed to remember 'the usual'?'*

William Scully, 1983

*'Funny, he managed to put Transubstantiation into a nutshell.
With the Bomb he's completely at sixes and sevens.'*

Martin Honeysett, 1983

*'Good movie. Want to hijack the plane now, or should
we wait until after dinner?'*

Bud Handelsman, 1983

Noel Ford, 1983

*'Just sell the tortoise, Jenkins.'*

Ken Pyne, 1983

Ed Fisher, 1983

'On the other hand, because of the biased and distorted reportage of Third World matters by the influential Western news media, maybe we only think life is lousy here!'

Bud Grace, 1983

'The practice of astrology took a major step towards achieving credibility today when, as predicted, everyone born under the sign of Scorpio was run over by an egg lorry.'

Tony Husband, 1985

'And where the hell have you been?'

David Haldane, 1983

'Oh no, the place has been ransacked!'

Harley Schwadron, 1983

'One look at you and I said, 'Now here's a guy who's not
going to fool around with silly opening one-liners'.'

William Scully, 1984

'Pity you so often go unread, Watkins. Your small print is masterly.'

Mike Williams, 1983

'Hey! I've just come up with a new idea for a football game.'

Larry (Terence Parkes), 1983

# LEMMINGS

Arcane and unfathomable fads swept the collective unconscious of *Punch* cartoonists. A Victorian fixation with organ grinders proliferated into manias for desert islands, hedgehogs and gurus in the twentieth century. But none are more inexplicable than the lemming craze of the early Eighties. Here are a few of the best, with Noel Ford's freefalling rodents flying in formation surely the greatest lemming cartoon of all time.

'It's the way he would have wanted it.'

BANX

Banx (Jeremy Banks), 1981

Noel Ford, 1980

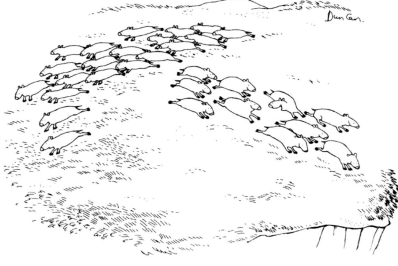

Riana Duncan, 1982

'Eamonn knows this amazing short cut.'

Nick Newman, 1983

*'You've got to hand it to them–they're adaptable little buggers.'*

John Whitfield Taylor, 1983

Martin Honeysett, 1982

*'We'll have to put these lemmings in a cage or something.'*

*'He'll wake up in a minute.'*

Riana Duncan, 1983

"Nobody calls Sir Rodney an idle bastard and gets away with it."

Peter Birkett, 1983

*'Not to worry, madam. This is a recurring dream in which I always wake up when we reach Cockfosters.'*

Roy Raymonde, 1983

*'Would you mind using the humane killer during working hours, Hodgkiss?'*

Noel Ford, 1083

Nick (Nicholas Hobart), 1983

*'...while those rats receiving B-12 shown quite remarkable initiative...'*

Ian Jackson, 1986

*'Don't be a fool, Mr Kilburn. Hand over the gerbil.'*

*'Secretly trained by the Americans? That's funny, so were we.'*

Ed Fisher, 1984

*'Terrible! You always think somehow that it can never happen to you.'*

Frank Cotham, 1984

*'I'm ten per cent lover, eight per cent poet and two per cent head librarian. the rest, I'm afraid, is water.'*

John Donegan, 1984

*'Just think — twenty years ago we'd both have been stuck in the kitchen.'*

Nick (Nicholas Hobart), 1984

Noel Ford, 1984

'What's our policy on the Nouveau Riche?'

Matt (Matthew Pritchett), 1988

'You must have seen a lot of change
since you began as a teacher.'

Bud Grace, 1984

'Now you're in big trouble. Here comes my solicitor.'

Noel Ford, 1984

'Are you expecting a case of agoraphobia?'

Banx (Jeremy Banks), 1982

'I still say there's got to be a catch somewhere.'

Harley Schwadron, 1984

'It's the family curse. Every full moon I turn into an accountant.'

William Scully, 1984

'Another instance of the folly of not breastfeeding.'

Holte (Trevor Holder), 1984

'It's good for a man to have a hobby.'

Merrily Harpur, 1982

'The secret of life is to snatch the fleeting moments of happiness between pre-menstrual tension and post-coital depression.'

Frank Cotham, 1984

'I love the absolute power that goes with my job. It allows me to be myself.'

Albert (Albert Rusling), 1984

'Neville agreed to settle out of court.'

Henry Martin, 1985

Frank Cotham, 1984

'I should like this memo to contain just a
slight hint of violence.'

Banx (Jeremy Banks), 1984

'There's usually four of us but Pestilence
is running in the 3.30 at Uttoxeter.'

David Langdon, 1987

'So it's a bright, sunny day with perhaps rain, fog, ice and snow, and moderate winds with a chance of reaching hurricane force...'

Nick (Nicholas Hobart), 1986

'How's the Psalms' title-page coming along?'

David Haldane, 1984

'It's OK. He's running our annual disco.'

Holte (Trevor Holder), 1985

'He said they give him a headache when he takes them out.'

Harley Schwadron, 1984

'I'm sorry, Mr Engstrom. Your way just doesn't add up.'

Sally Artz, 1984

'Strange to think a whole generation has grown up knowing
nothing of matching accessories.'

Banx (Jeremy Banks), 1984

'...However we're not being paid to
'Live and Let Live', Hargreaves.'

Holte (Trevor Holder), 1984

'Don't worry, the wife won't be back from her macrame, or
origami, or whatever the hell she's studying these days.'

Bud Handelsman, 1984

'What a nightmare! I've taken a whole party of people to
'Carmen', at £40 a seat, and Placido Domingo can't remember
how 'Cette fleur que tu m'avais jetée' goes.'

'Our spells have never been the same
since we got the bleedin' wok.'

'I see the Hitachi deal fell through.'

'Pens!'

Holte (Trevor Holder), 1985

'I think we're all agreed then – Blend 79 just about has it all.'

Albert (Albert Rusling), 1985

'A few years ago you never saw a fox in the suburbs.'

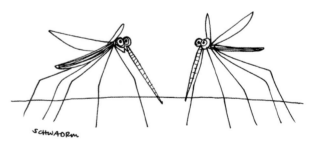

Harley Schwadron, 1986

'Come on, it's a Saturday night. Let's go
find a drunk and have a good time.'

John Donegan, 1985

'You're kidding! Just that and they feed you?'

Ian Jackson, 1985

Henry Martin, 1986

*'Happy birthday to you! Happy birthday to you!*
*Happy birthday, dear Foofoo, Happy birthday to you!'*

Stan McMurtry, 1985

*'Stop moaning – we were at **your** parents' last year!'*

David Haldane, 1985

*'Hello, folks, this is your Captain speaking. May I introduce my best friend,
Boko? Boko flies the aeroplane when I'm not feeling well.'*

John Whitfield Taylor, 1985

*'Charlie Jackson's daughter only charges four
pounds an hour for tuition.'*

Henry Martin, 1985

*'Listen pal, if you're not entirely satisfied, bring it
back and we'll put another one over on you.'*

Bud Grace, 1985

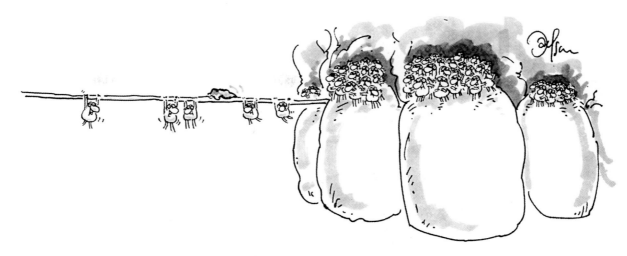

Ian Jackson, 1985

'Remember the good old days before dental-floss?'

Harley Schwadron, 1985

'Myron is in that awkward period
between fuddy and duddy.'

Banx (Jeremy Banks), 1986

SHANGRI-LA
TWINNED WITH
BURNLEY

- 519 -

Pete Dredge, 1983

'Can I borrow the car tonight, Dad?'

Holte (Trevor Holder), 1984

'Sorry about that – he's allergic to cats.'

Ed Fisher, 1983

*'It was 1961. Boom times, stability, easy credit...and, of course, none of the other entering classmen at law school thought of specialising in insolvency cases.'*

Banx (Jeremy Banks), 1983

*'The first thing you've got to do is get over feeling self-conscious.'*

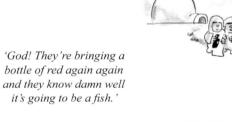

*'God! They're bringing a bottle of red again again and they know damn well it's going to be a fish.'*

Chic (Cyril Alfred Jacob), 1988

Bud Grace, 1983

*'Bloody hell, Mavis! The bus leaves in ten minutes.'*

Nick Newman, 1987

*'Strewth, Norm – you look like you've just seen a ghost!'*

# HANDELSMAN FREAKY FABLES

*Horatio and Emma*

or, The Frail Hero

**THE NILE: DESTRUCTION OF NAPOLEON'S NAVY**

Take that, French fries! Egypt shall be forever British!

Zut!

Très zut!

BOOM

As an Egyptian, I resent this. Pass it on.

**NAPLES: FORTUNE-TELLING AT THE HAMILTONS'**

Sir Nelson, you will fall in love with Lady Ham—oh, **sorry**.

Great fleet! Just what I was thinking myself!

Me too!

We cannot escape our fate, Emma — **ow**.

My own Horatio! Oh, **sorry**.

Well, Hardy?

You are recalled to active duty, sir.

Absolutely not! Doctor's orders! Can't you see the man is **wounded**?

**LONDON: CONFRONTATION AT THE NELSONS'**

Really, my dear Fanny, there is no reason to be jealous! You have refinement and elegance, while Lady H. here is as common as dirt.

That's quite true, Mrs N.

For my part, Mrs N, I am proud to be cuckolded by such a hero! Land of ho-ope and glory…

**COPENHAGEN: THE FAMOUS TELESCOPE INCIDENT**

The enemy are signalling their desire to surrender to your lordship's ladyship.

What?

**MERTON**

Well, Hardy?

It's the French again, sir.

Stay and fight **me**! What have the French got that I ain't?

**PORTSMOUTH**

…for he's a jolly good handicapped person…

I warn you, Horatio — if you get killed, I'm leaving you.

For heaven's sake, Emma, there go my front teeth.

**TRAFALGAR: REDESTRUCTION OF NAPOLEON'S NAVY**

England suspects that every man may screw his cutie… No, that's not it… England inspects that…

Chacun à son goût!

Idée fixe!

BOOM

Je me lève! Je vais au tableau noir!

Well, Hardy?

And give you my cold? I'd never forgive myself.

**MORAL:** Only the brave can stand the fair.

Bud Handelsman, 1983

*"Don't touch the Stilton,' I said. 'It'll only trigger off your migraine."*

*'Here we go, Winston – exercise time.'*

*'I am sorry – I would have sent you a Valentine,
but you see how it is...'*

Martin Ross, 1991

'Honey, I can't seem to get through to Rentokil.'

Harley Schwadron, 1986

'You'll hate California.'

Henry Martin, 1986

'Look out! Ready or not, here I come! Gangway!'

John Donegan, 1984

'Go and see what's bothering him. He doesn't usually howl for nothing.'

'No! He's my pal!'

Charles Barsotti, 1988

'I planted Iris this year. Next year I think
I'll plant her mother.'

Bud Grace, 1986

'We're not taking this very seriously, are we?'

David Haldane, 1986

- 524 -

'Fetch me the law for the rich, will you?'

Riana Duncan, 1986

COMPUTER
SALES

'Just show me the mouse.'

Harley Schwadron, 1985

Robert Thompson, 1991

'Joyce, this coffee's bitter.'

John Donegan, 1986

'I'm none too proud of that one. He thought I was taking his picture.'

Ed McLachlan, 1982

'There are two sides to every argument, George, and I've already presented them both.'

Riana Duncan, 1986

Charles Barsotti, 1987

'Whatever it turns out to be, rush it to production.'

John Donegan, 1987

'Of course, Margaret working is a great help. She buys all her own gin.'

Harley Schwadron, 1986

'Sorry to be the bearer of bad tidings, Thigben, but your
retirement was a computer error.'

Frank Cotham, 1986

'I want you to go to the Personnel Director and bite
him, then go to Sales and bite Hempstead and Beasly,
then trot on down to Bookkeeping...'

Jonathan Pugh, 1991

'The market's never been better for the first-time buyer.'

Roy Raymonde, 1988

'We've been refused planning permission!'

Michael ffolkes (Brian Davis), 1988

'Sanctuary! I'm escaping advertising.'

Cluff (John Longstaff), 1988

'Well, gentlemen, we've got a stunning new logo and a marvellous publicity
campaign ready. We just need to come up with a product.'

Adam John Singleton, 1991

John Donegan, 1986

'Well, at least I got one thing right.
Money was everything.'

Ken Allen, 1988

'I live in constant fear of being robbed by
the Government.'

Les Barton, 1988

'My goodness, getting mad won't help.'

Ed McLachlan, 1980

'They've mugged the Pearly King, Inspector, but he
must have put up a hell of a struggle.'

Banx (Jeremy Banks), 1982

'I just live for the day when we catch those
Roman bastards at it, that's all.'

Riana Duncan, 1988

'I'm going out to lunch, Miss Wilson. Fight off any takeover bids that may occur while I'm away.'

Matt (Matthew Pritchett), 1989

Banx (Jeremy Banks), 1986

William Scully, 1986

'Here comes the waiter. Oh good! It's the one who pretends to understand your French.'

Frank Cotham, 1986

'You're the psychologist, Frisbane. Is this danger real or imagined?'

'It's a funny thing but it's not adult conversation
I crave so much as the mindless repetition of
office tittle-tattle...'

Merrily Harpur, 1980

Eli (Eli Bauer), 1988

Neil Bennett, 1991

'You'll have to excuse Dorothy – it's that time of the month.'

Peter Birkett, 1988

Bud Grace, 1986

'Need I remind you, gentlemen, that we're here to study anatomy?'

Ray Lowry, 1986

'I had a few good years in Edward Hopper's pictures. Then – nothing!'

EARTH MOTHER

come on, you little sods

Pearsall

'He's a lousy provider but, boy, can he kiss.'

- 533 -

'Let me get this straight, your honour – do you want the
truth, the whole truth or nothing but the truth?'

# PETER BIRKETT

The cartoonists' favourite cartoonist, Peter Birkett was responsible for one of *Punch's* best-loved cartoons of the twentieth century – the bumbling Daleks whose plans to conquer the Universe are thwarted by a flight of stairs (*see* page 469). His first cartoon for *Punch* appeared in 1969, the majority appearing in the early 1980s and though his output was low, nearly every one was a winner. His squat, immediately recognisable figures exist in a surreal universe all Birkett's own.

Peter Birkett, 1982

'Personally, Sargeant, I'd say suicide – but I think we're going to need a psychiatrist's report.'

Peter Birkett, 1981

'That's Olmroyd, the lucky blighter – he's excused Poetry.'

Peter Birkett, 1992

'Remember, this is an important interview –
I'll do the talking.'

*'You've been fighting again!'*

Peter Birkett, 1981

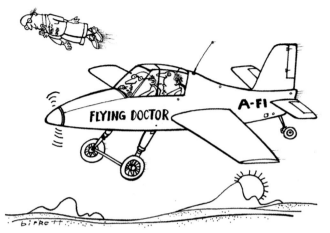

*'It's that bloody faith-healer again!'*

Peter Birkett, 1981

*'There must be more to the After-life than hanging around the British Museum.'*

Peter Birkett, 1982

*'Actually, there was a vacancy, but it was filled a few minutes ago.'*

Peter Birkett, 1982

Holte (Trevor Holder), 1987

*'Forget the crêpe Suzette, Minchin – I'll have the rice-pudding.'*

**- 536**

Eli (Eli Bauer), 1987

*'I'll take them!'*

Robert Thompson, 1991

*'Bless you.'*

Ian Jackson, 1987

*'The best parties always end up in the kitchen.'*

*'It's The Wild again.'*

John Donegan, 1987

Frank Cotham, 1986

David Haldane, 1988

*'The dog's being impossible again.'*

John Donegan, 1987

'My family's all grown up now –
except my husband, of course.'

Frank Cotham, 1987

'What's the matter, dear? Cat got your tongue?'

JUMP, BOY!

GOD, YOUR LIFE
MUST BE DULL.

Charles Barsotti 1988

Ed McLachlan, 1987

'Where's that waiter with our fish course?'

Tony Reeve, 1987

'Trust me – enigmatic is better.'

Harley Schwadron, 1987

'Why, I used to lie around and sleep all day, too,
but that was before I discovered caffeine.'

Henry Martin, 1987

'I dreamt that a seat-belt law for pets was
passed, Muffin wouldn't comply and I was sent
to Sing Sing for two years of hard labour.'

Bill Stott, 1987

'Have you had any thoughts about
what it might be worth?'

David Haldane, 1987

'Oh, he won't bother with this lot. He only burns first editions.'

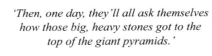

'Then, one day, they'll all ask themselves how those big, heavy stones got to the top of the giant pyramids.'

Harley Schwadron, 1987

Martin Honeysett, 1987

'I said, we must have lunch some time.'

David Hawker, 1983

'...and then suddenly the sun breaks through and their human rights record doesn't seem so bad at all.'

Ian Jackson, 1987

'Steward's enquiry? What steward's enquiry?'

Banx (Jeremy Banks), 1984

'Them? They're just a bunch of bloody students.'

Bill Stott, 1087

'Your hearing-aid, you twisted, miserable old ratbag.'

Matt (Matthew Pritchett), 1988

Holte (Trevor Holder), 1987

'Amazin' stuff! Can't understand why they took it off the market –
I mean, just look at the size of those Brassicas!'

David Langdon, 1988

'Sorry, madam – the
chef says he cannot
reveal his sauces.'

William Scully, 1988

'Let's get moving. I'm beginning to feel
like an advert for a pension fund.'

'Hold back, Rusty – it's too obvious. It could be a trap.'

- 543 -

'You're an ecosystem and I'm an ecosystem.
Anything that has fleas is an ecosystem.'

'Permission to write a poem, sir?'

'We're planning a small dinner party. Do you have any
vegetables no one's heard of yet?'

Riana Duncan, 1988

'That's an excellent suggestion, Miss Triggs. Perhaps
one of the men here would like to make it.'

Mike Williams, 1981

'Wow! I must paint this up when I get home.'

Arthur Reid, 1988

'The big problem with your illness, Mr Hawkins, is that nobody
famous has caught it yet.'

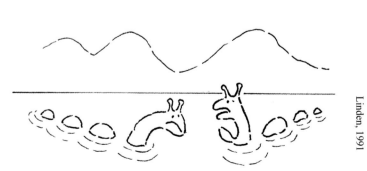

Linden, 1991

'Look, you've got to believe in yourself.'

*'I'm sorry, Maisie. I've been turning on the charm all day. I need a rest.'*

William Scully, 1988

Robert Thompson, 1991

*'We can't. It would spoil our working relationship.'*

Sam Smith, 1988

*'Scope for advancement? I'll say. Take me, for instance.
I first came to this store as shoplifter.'*

Ken Pyne, 1988

*'I've always been a one-man woman,
Gerald, and for the past four years it hasn't been you.'*

Ray Lowry, 1988

'Adrian doesn't do anything – he's creative.'

Matt (Matthew Pritchett), 1988

'How about coming back to my place, cooking supper,
putting the kids to bed and ironing me a shirt?'

Steve Way, 1988

'I hate private views.'

Bill Stott, 1988

'This one's useless – it keeps going, 'Oh, God, say it's only a dream.
Oh, God, say it's only a dream'.'

Jan van Wessum, 1988

'You've been sleepwalking again.'

Frank Cotham, 1988

'They're on to us!'

Ed McLachlan, 1988

'Mmm, I just love to run my fingers
through a man's wallet.'

John Donegan, 1989

'Never mind 'Pourquoi?' – just get it!'

Pete Dredge, 1988

Eli (Eli Bauer), 1988

Neil Bennett, 1989

- 548 -

'Mr McGregor's got a Flymo!'

Henry Martin, 1976

Les Barton, 1989

Harley Schwadron, 1988

'They say their lives are in danger if they go back!'

'Everything in this house is non-fattening.
How come we're fat?'

Patricia Drennan, 1988

'Good heavens, Dorian – how dreadful!'

Frank Cotham, 1988

'You're noisy for a cat.'

Cluff (John Longstaff), 1988

'A table for four incredibly obese, offensive, yet extremly rich bastards!'

Nick Newman, 1984

'It's party time!'

Bud Handelsman, 1982

'There goes another one. What do you say?
Shall we seize power?'

Robert Thompson, 1991

'It's so peaceful, I bet you can hear my car
alarm across six valleys.'

David Haldane, 1985

'We must get rid of him, Father.
He puts garlic in everything.'

Albert (Albert Rusling), 1982

'Ah! Here comes the custard now.'

Banx (Jeremy Banks), 1981

'The trick is to get the Continental Drift behind you.'

William Scully, 1982

'First the magic went out of my marriage, now it's gone out of my Volvo.'

# MICHAEL HEATH

## B.1935

Recorder of the zeitgeist, du Maurier on speed, Heath focused his sharp eye on fashionable London – its demi-monde, chattering classes and brash City wide-boys. Heath first started contributing to *Punch* in 1958; by the mid-Sixties he had found his niche as satirist of the neuroses, fads and sexual politics of the age. Many of his best cartoons illustrated 'Metropolis', Alan Brien's column on London. Here he offers a brilliant illustrated diary of his week for another *Punch* feature of the Seventies, 'Strictly Personal'.

1.

*While at 'Punch' I'm asked to draw diary.*

*Draw up cartoon in same office as Jak and Frank Dickens*

4.

*People still upset about cartoon I did the day Victor the giraffe died.*

HAVE I GOT A STORY FOR YOU THIS WILL BLOW THE LID OFF.....

WHY DON'T WE DO A 'GREAT BORE' ABOUT A CARTOONIST WHO DRAWS ABOUT HIMSELF IN "PUNCH"

7.

2.

Start the week dreaming up my cartoon for 'Evening Standard'.

*Deliver roughs to Simon Jenkins. He liked one (thank God!)*

3.

Lawyer objects, have to do another!

5.

Rush off to 'The Spectator' who are kind enough to ask me to lunch.

6.

Lunch with Graham Greene and Germaine Greer, feel inadequate as Germaine is cross between Max Miller and Henry Miller.

- 553 -

8.

Later go for a drink with Jeffrey Bernard in the French (York Minster) pub in Soho.

9.

Arrive home.

Michael Heath, 1977

'Oh wow! A stretch zimmer.'

Ray Lowry, 1989

'No doubt you've heard about my
reputation as a bit of a man-eater.'

Tony Husband, 1989

Ken Allen, 1989

Stan Eales, 1989

Neil Bennett, 1989

Frank Cotham, 1989

'My plan is this: at sunset I start miaowing like crazy and
the guards put me out for the night.'

- 556 -

'My relaxation at weekends
is a regional accent.'

'Relax. He's in a good mood.'

Henry Martin, 1989

'Okay, everybody. Ready for the annual report?
Start spinning. Willard, your high tech empire has
been taken over by a Japanese conglomerate. Edna,
your Miss Perfect child, Emily, is centre-stage in a
religious/sex scandal. Arvin, honour student Arvin,
Jr, was tossed out of Harvard for dealing crack...'

Riana Duncan, 1988

'Our Ron is always doing things for other people. At the moment
he's helping the police with their enquiries.'

- 557 -

Adam John Singleton, 1990

'Hello, Samaritans? It's me again...'

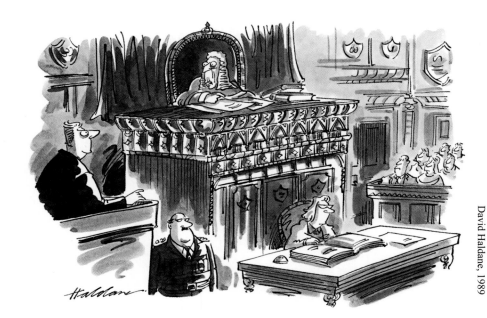

David Haldane, 1989

'Ernest Pringle, alias Ernie the hypnotist, I sentence you to three
months in Barbados, all expenses paid.'

Tony Husband, 1989

'That reminds me – the strap broke on ours.
I must get it repaired.'

Ed McLachlan, 1988

'The British still say the death sentence against
Salman Rushdie is unacceptable – but would you
consider Jeffrey Archer instead?'

Ken Pyne, 1989

'I'm afraid he still hasn't quite mastered the new technology.'

Henry Martin, 1985

'Frankly, Wallace, I think you'd better stop telling
it. If no one laughs, it may not be a joke.'

Bud Grace, 1986

'Actually, I'm not really Cupid. Hand over your wallet.'

BEEP! BEEP!
BEEP! BEEP!
BEEP! BEEP!
BEEP!

David Haldane, 1989

'And Clive will always be remembered as the most
hard-working member of the sales team.'

William Haefeli, 1980

'It seems we were lulled into a false sense
of security by non-fat frozen yoghurt.'

*'There used to be a small yellow bird perched on his nose but it was covered over in Victorian times.'*

*'Good morning, sir. The Bureau of Statistics is conducting an inter-regional survey into how many men actually use the little slot in their Y-fronts, and wonder if you'd like to help.'*

'It's dead easy, just land on that ship and explode.'

- 561 -

'Your complete ignorance on every other subject
is only matched by your detailed knowledge of
each provision on corporal punishment by the
European Court of Human Rights.'

'Well, Mr Mackenzie, it says nothing in your CV about ponytails.'

Mike Williams, 1989

Tony Husband, 1989

'Yes?'

Ed McLachlan, 1990

*'Look at my bloody beans! Covered in bloody aphids! I'd like to
know what the bloody ladybirds are feeding on!'*

'Now, if you had £50 worth of crack in your pocket and you mugged an old lady who had £35...'

'This is Hodgkinson – he's in charge of the shredder.'

'I have this fear of inadvertently drifting into satire!'

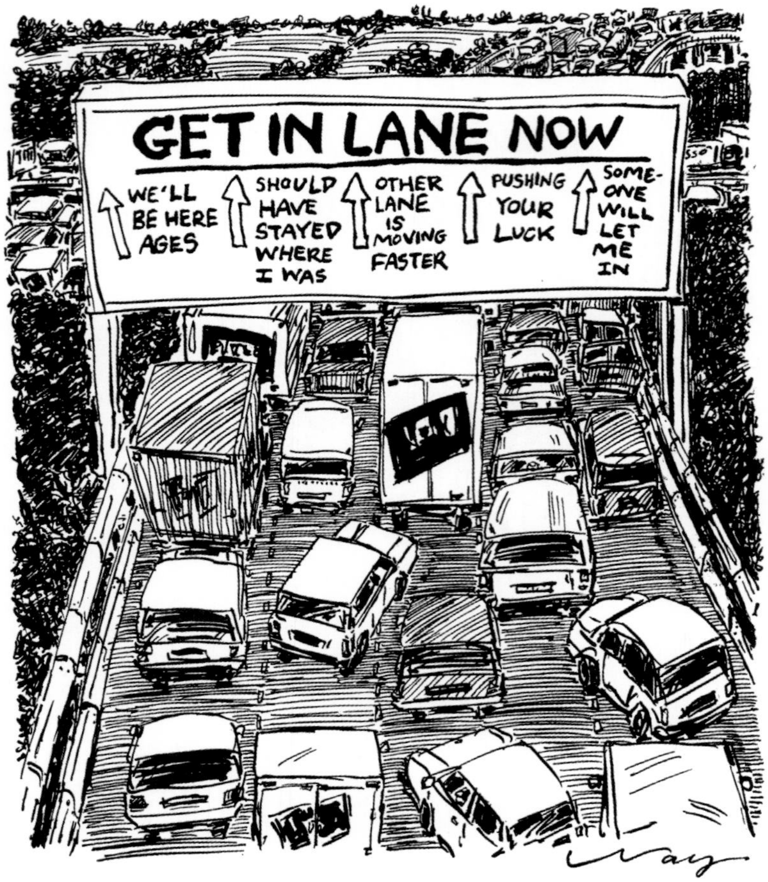
GET IN LANE NOW
WE'LL BE HERE AGES
SHOULD HAVE STAYED WHERE I WAS
OTHER LANE IS MOVING FASTER
PUSHING YOUR LUCK
SOME-ONE WILL LET ME IN
Way

Steve Way, 1989

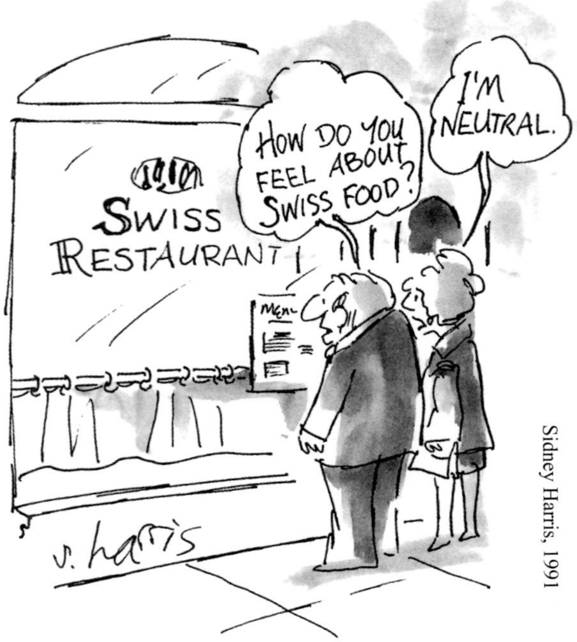
SWISS RESTAURANT
MENU
HOW DO YOU FEEL ABOUT SWISS FOOD?
I'M NEUTRAL.
S. Harris

Sidney Harris, 1991



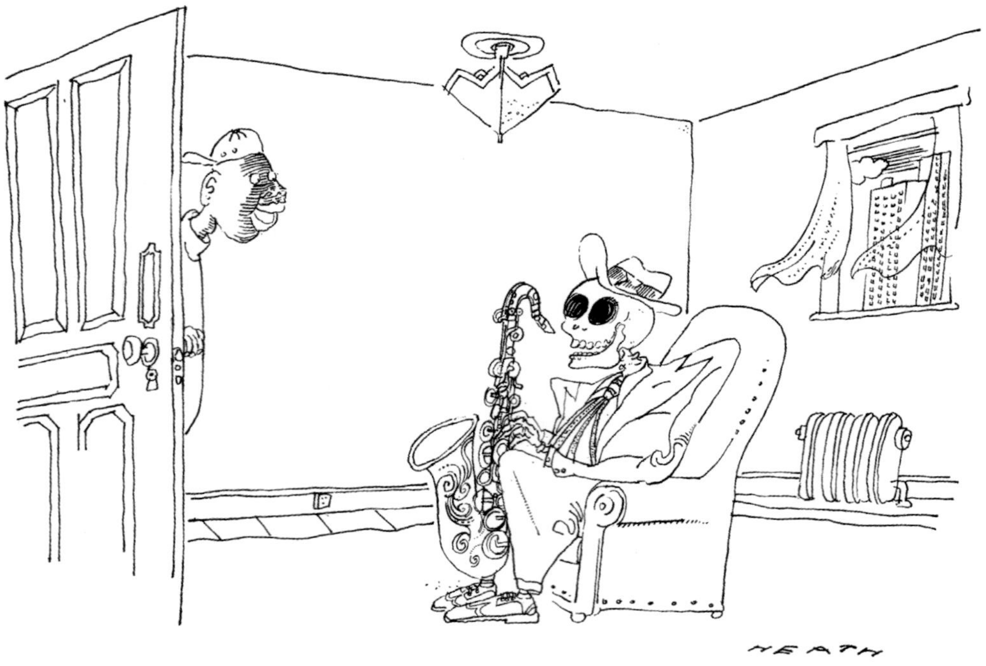
HEATH

*'Jazz is back!'*

Michael Heath, 1986

William Scully, 1990

'Be patient. The violence will be restored very shortly.'

Ken Pyne, 1989

'To be honest, I only joined the party in the hope of being embroiled in a sex scandal.'

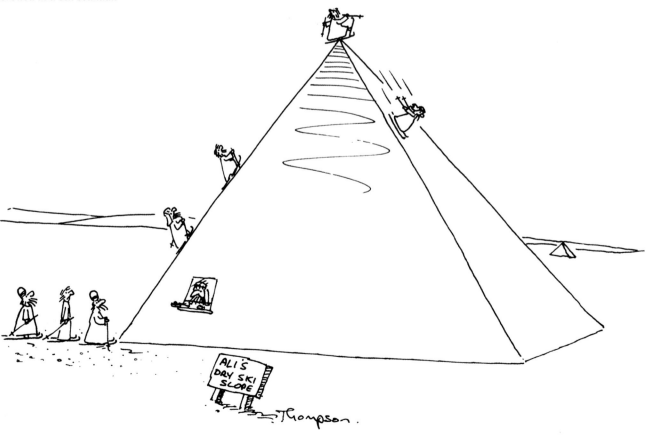

Geoff Thompson, 1987

Ken Allen, 1990

John Jensen, 1990

Ken Pyne, 1990

*'It's Gerald's way of getting round the hosepipe ban.'*

'Nothing personal, Pooh, but we've figured you'd fetch a fortune on the open market.'

'Bloody hell, it's another stair-carpet salesman!'

'So it's agreed. We support your claim to the throne if you appear on our shortbread tins.'

'Actually, we wanted a cat. But not
many cats fetch and carry.'

Les Barton, 1990

'Gee, I dunno – those clouds look threatening.'

Nick Downes, 1990

Nick (Nicholas Hobart), 1986

Noel Ford, 1990

'Tragic case – three years ago he forgot his PIN number.'

Frank Cotham, 1986

'For heaven's sake, Hempstead – perk up!'

Martin Ross, 1990

'Whoops, must get that laser fixed.'

Ray Lowrey, 1990

'This is serious – even Shit Creek's up shit creek.'

Riana Duncan, 1986

'Fetch me the law for the rich, will you?'

John Donegaan, 1986

'There's a furry thing in here eating cheese.
I understand that's your department.'

Bud Grace, 1986

"Now what?"

'Now what?'

Neil Bennett, 1990

'I'm awarding you a GCSE. It doesn't entitle you
to drive, but it avoids the stigma of failure.'

Sidney Harris, 1986

Martin Ross, 1992

Michael Heath, 1987

'He has your greed, darling.'

Martin Honeysett, 1986

'It's clues we're looking for, constable.'

Riana Duncan, 1985

'Leave me if you must, Marjorie, but to run away with
my best friend, that's what really hurts.'

David Myers, 1991

'Now I want a straight answer – that didn't get there by itself.'

'For God's sake we must
think of something to
talk about — we're the
chattering classes'

Ken Pyne, 1991

Robert Thompson, 1992

'Sorry, Nuk. Not much of a fly-past.'

Charles Barsotti, 1987

David Haldane, 1982

*'Kids! They'll do anything to draw attention to themselves.'*

Martin Honeysett, 1990

*'The doctor's busy. Do you want your ear syringed or not?'*

Martin Ross, 1991

*'Sometimes I wish it had killed me outright.'*

William Haefeli, 1990

*'I'm sorry – what's your name again? when you told me I had no
reason to believe I'd want to remember.'*

Les Barton, 1991

Tony Reeve, 1992

Bud Handelsman, 1990

'Hey, let's not underestimate science! I bet they're working on a replacement to the ozone layer right now.'

William Scully, 1990

'My first husband may have had countless shortcomings, but my goodness, he could always find somewhere to park.'

William Haefeli, 1990

'It doesn't matter what outfit you buy. Ten years from now you'll look back on it and think it made you look goofy.'

David Myers, 1990

'It took time but we finally got him house-trained.'

Noel Ford, 1990

'Buy a copy of Watchtower and we'll
unclamp your car.'

Ed McLachlan, 1990

'Really, Mr Casey! What sort of English teacher is it that doesn't know
the difference between corporal and capital punishment?!'

Mike Williams, 1991

'Why so gloomy, Olaf?'

Ken Pyne, 1990

*'I tell you! No one's gonna take away my British identity!'*

David Myers, 1990

*'I think they want to go walkies.'*

William Haefeli, 1990

*'I'm not afraid of commitment. I'm afraid of you.'*

Ray Lowry, 1990

*'It's my protest against the plight of the homeless and destitute. A limited, signed
edition of cardboard boxes, hand cast in bronze and available at £5,000 each.'*

John Donegan, 1987

'Winnie the what?'

Sidney Harris, 1990

Ed Fisher, 1990

'But we can't invite ONLY your
imaginary friends to your party.'

'Remember, men, the enemy will be facing you
in cheap ready-to-wears; you'll be fighting
them in uniforms designed by Michelangelo.'

Neil Bennett, 1991

*'It's Mother Teresa! She's got compassion fatigue!'*

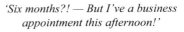

Noel Ford, 1991

*'Six months?! — But I've a business
appointment this afternoon!'*

William Haefeli, 1991

*'I wish you'd hold my hand or something. It would help clarify
our relationship for the benefit of casual passers-by.'*

Les Barton, 1992

Clive Collins 1991

'I'm sorry. I don't make house calls...'

Pete Williams, 1991

THANK YOU FOR NOT DELIVERING BROWN ENVELOPES.

WAR AND PEACE

Harley Schwadron, 1991

Satoshi (Satoshi Kambayashi), 1991

'Cut! The goldfish is overacting!'

Tony Husband 1991

'Oh that...Nothing a little Polyfilla couldn't solve.'

'Mum has this belief that he's going to come back as a goldfish.'

Ken Pyne, 1991

LITTLE ROCK
DEATH
TO ALL WHO ENTER.

'Looks like the kind of place a guy
could settle down, find a woman,
learn to read.'

Robert Thompson, 1991

- 580 -

CONDOMS

Ian Jackson, 1990

MARVO'S
FLEA
CIRCUS...

VET

'We're trying to raise him to be too polite to verbalise any of the
prejudices we've taught him.'

William Haefeli, 1990

'I'm sorry, but he'd broken a leg.'

David Myers, 1990

Richard Burnie, 1991

*'I've told you, I'm not a witch,*
*I'm an aromatherapist.'*

David Haldane, 1989

*'I don't give a damn who you are,*
*stop trying to talk me out of it!'*

Neil Bennett, 1991

*'Bugger Equal Opportunities –*
*I still say she should mind the house!'*

Martin Ross, 1991

*'I think, initially, we should clear up the issue of*
*what can and cannot be treated by homeopathy.'*

Mike Williams, 1990

*'Well, that's the last of the Mohicans. There's still*
*a bit of Sioux left, if anyone's interested.'*

'They'll be unbearable when they get the swimming pool.'

Mike Williams, 1983

Robert Thompson, 1991

'I'm going for a personal worst.'

Albert (Albert Rusling), 1985

'Solicitors can make a lot of money. Yes, if I were you I'd mug a solicitor.'

Ed McLachlan, 1987

'I don't like the look of this!'

'Do you have one with fewer buttons.'

'By the way, I'd like to compliment you on being one of the
few women who look good in horizontal stripes.'

- 583 -

'Holy recession, Batman. It's not the same
since we lost our company car.'

'I'm meeting the English cricket team.'

'Greetings! Male bonding over there. Male bashing over here.'

# TONY HUSBAND

## B.1950

Often outrageous, never politically correct, always funny – one of *Punch*'s rude boys – Tony Husband became a star in the mid-Eighties. A self-taught artist who became a full-time freelancer in 1984, Husband has gone on to become a multiple award-winning cartoonist, with more than fifteen books to his name in the UK and ten in Germany, where he has a huge following.

*'Nothing personal, Mr. Knight, but I was hoping to speak to one of the others.'*

Tony Husband, 1989

Tony Husband, 1991

*'Oi! Can't you read?'*

Tony Husband, 1989

*'That was funny when he said he'd get his big brother.'*

Tony Husband, 1989

'I'm desperate for a cause.'

Tony Husband, 1990

'Wow! She can test my eyes any time.'

Tony Husband, 1989

'He was okay with the sex and drugs. It was
the rock 'n' roll that finished him.'

Tony Husband, 1992

Tony Husband, 1991

'Where did we meet? Now there's a story.'

McArdle, 1991

Pete Dredge, 1991

'Hurry up with the camcorder, Colin!
Grandad's about to go under.'

Pete Williams, 1991

- 586 -

'Mother's Day isn't much of a time for cuckoos...'

Sewell (Patricia Carter), 1991

'... it means we don't deliver.'

Martin Honeysett, 1991

'How's the novel coming on?'

Robert Thompson, 1991

'Must be a pointer.'

Bestie (Steven Best), 1991

Nick (Nicholas Hobart), 1991

'Roger, tell them about our travel insurance.'

Bud Handelsman, 1991

Ray Lowry, 1990

'He says if he concentrates hard enough he can remember the
golden age of the Punch cartoon.'

David Myers, 1990

'How much should I put in?'

Bud Handelsman, 1991

'When Daddy tells you how much he's worth, it means that's how much he has. Daddy as such has practically no market value.'

Robert Thompson, 1991

'Look, maybe a candlelit dinner wasn't such a good idea.'

Nick (Nicholas Hobart), 1991

'Are you sure this is a hostile takeover?'

Simon Meyrick-Jones, 1991

'I think we should keep the same policies, but change the logo.'

Neil Bennett, 1991

'I must say, I find the introverts less threatening.'

Pete Williams, 1991

'The West ain't as wild as it used to be.'

Martin Ross, 1991

Tony Reeve, 1991

Ken Pyne, 1991

'Oh my God! We've had social workers!'

Charles Barsotti, 1988

'Hello, Sainsbury's? Do you sell dog food for very naughty
puppies? No? Well I certainly don't blame you. Thank you,
Sainsbury's and goodbye.'

*'Rabid, my foot! He's just been for a pint.'*

*'And this is us getting the tube to Heathrow.'*

*'Believe me, kid - in ten minutes you'll be able to climb* **through** *the goddamn looking-glass.'*

*'Conventional or unconventional wisdom?'*

Michael Heath, 1984

'Have you tried drink?

Neil Bennett, 1990

Ed McLachlan, 1991

Rakesh (Rakesh Sahgal), 1991

'This one has a free anti-depressant.'

K (Mike Kelly), 1991

Martin Ros, 1991

'Hmmm, minature lights, minature speakers—
it all begins to make sense.'

Neil Bennett, 1991

'Designed by mixed
ability architects.'

- 592 -

Martin Honetsett, 1985

'More glue, vicar?'

William Haefeli, 1992

'OK, so I'm not the man you thought I was.
Is it my fault you're a lousy judge of character?'

Tony Reeve, 1992

Ian Jackson, 1984

'Well, Piglet, that's the last we'll see of
his ruddy computer.'

Tom Cheney, 1991

- 593 -

'Please...I don't want to hear anymore about your rotten childhood.'

Ray Lowry, 1991

'New Country night. They all stand around crying into their Perrier water!'

Simon Meyrick-Jones, 1991

'I'll thank you not to discuss our
relationship with total strangers.'

Adam John Singleton, 1991

*'And folklore has it they never forget...'*

Simon Meyrick-Jones, 1991

*'It's Ken. He's been like it since since he split up with Barbie.'*

Sewell (Patricia Carter), 1991

*'Amanda tells me you cook. I eat.'*

Les Barton, 1992

Martin Ross, 1991

'It's a bit rough in here.'

Harley Schwadron, 1982

'That's right. We've moved Mr. Robinson from the intensive care unit to the insensitive no-one gives a damn unit.'

Ken Allen, 1992

- 595 -

'Oh no! We've got mice!'

William Haefeli, 1991

'When you accepted our dinner invitation you implictly signed a contract agreeing to eat whatever food we chose to serve you.'

Neil Bennett, 1991

'It's a serial killer, Sarge – he wants Mr Bun the baker for the set.'

Pete Dredge, 1992

'It'll have to be retaken – the keeper moved!'

Martin Ross, 1992

'I'm just ahead of my time, that's the problem.'

Martin Honeysett, 1991

'Bit of a rough game today I'm afraid, Mrs. Titmarsh.'

Mike Williams, 1991

Tony Husband, 1992

'What are you wagging your tail at you cheerful bastard?'

Noel Ford, 1986

Roy Raymonde, 1981

'Well, well! Remember
that? My pedestal!'

Tony Reeve, 1992

'Well, son — love is a very special thing
which happens between a drummer and
six or seven groupies.'

Pete Williams, 1991

PETS

£12
SLIGHTLY
SHOP SOILED

£9
SLIGHTLY
SHOP SOILED

SALE

£6
SLIGHTLY
SHOP SOILED

£4
SLIGHTLY
SOILED THE
SHOP

£8
SLIGHTLY
SH

£10
SLIGHTLY
SHOP SOILED

Ken Pyne, 1991

'I think I should have warned you - Brian's not a passive smoker.'

You're a deeply unpleasant person Mrs Feldmar, but give me three years and I can prove it isn't your fault

Gray Joliffe, 1991

Tony Reeve, 1992

Robert Thompson, 1992

'Smoking them's not too bad, it's putting them out with your foot that really hurts.'

Martin Honeysett, 1992

'Don't worry, the au pair will clean it up.'

Simon Meyrick-Jones, 1991

'He's getting a babysitter. That means our days as a fashion accessory are over.'

Pete Dredge, 1990

'I'm the lager waiter, chief!'

Ken Allen, 1989

'We'd like to try for a 'Baby on Board' sign.'

Nick (Nicholas Hobart), 1992

'Margaret's off sick. I'm the temp.'

in assocation with

POWERGEN

Neil Bennett, 1991

# MIKE WILLIAMS

## B.1940

The twentieth century's Charles Keene (but with better gags), Mike Williams is a true master of technique – his current pen of choice is a seagull's feather picked up on the beach near his home. One of the celebrated alumni of Quarry Bank High School in Liverpool (a contemporary was John Lennon), Williams began cartooning for *Punch* in 1967. Putting historical characters from Walter Raleigh to Hitler into perspective is a favourite theme. As John Cleese wrote about Williams' work: 'If these cartoons don't make you laugh out loud, you must be Swiss (or dead).'

Mike Williams, 1976

'The hell with the Costa del Sol – why don't we all go to the Bahamas?'

Mike Williams, 1981

'One of the really nice things about the Spring is being able to turn the central heating down a little.'

Mike Williams, 1972

'Big deal! You ought to try **papering** a ceiling sometime!'

Mike Williams, 1983

'I am Igsprx from the planet Thynog–take me to your toilet.'

Mike Williams, 1983

'They must be nearly ready to sail.'

Mike Williams, 1981

Mike Williams, 1991

Nick Downes, 1989

'Could that be our Ritchie tinkling on the piano?'

Harley Schwadron, 1992

'It's your birthday? Cook anything you want for supper.'

'You can always tell the Poms
– they peel terribly!'

Ken Pyne, 1991

WARNING
SHOPLIFTERS

The merchandise
in this store is
not as valuable as
our prices indicate

William Haefeli, 1991

Martin Ross, 1991

'I anticipate a coup by an old hardliner and
loss of democratic remote control.'

Robert Thomson, 1991

'People try to put us down...'

David Brown, 1991

Tony Husband, 1991

'You know, it's nice to go travelling
but it's oh so nice to come home.'

Stan Eales, 1989

- 603 -

'Come on in...the water's horrible.'

Henry Martin, 1986

'Mr. Jalton, I think we're about to be wooed by Apex Ltd.'

Riana Duncan, 1984

'Well, tell the doctor to come over quickly. Mr. Braithwaite
has lost the will to argue.'

'Winter time, I generally warm the milking machine.'

Bud Grace, 1983

'I haven't felt this important in years.'

Ken Pyne, 1991

'It's that fat jock again – this time tell him he'll be
manager of Glasgow Rangers.'

Pete Williams, 1991

VAL D'ISÈRE TRAVEL

VISIT CROYDON

HOLIDAYS IN CLAPHAM

WINTER BREAKS IN BASINGSTOKE

FLY/DRIVE TO SLOUGH

TOUR PECKHAM

Nick Newman, 1992

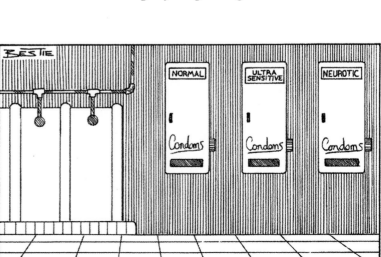

BESTIE

NORMAL

ULTRA SENSITIVE

NEUROTIC

Condoms

Condoms

Condoms

Bestie (Steve Best), 1992

'Bad news, I'm afraid. Our artistic licence has expired!'

Ray Lowry, 1991

'On the other hand, if you're looking for
something more durable...'

Tom Cheney, 1991

'We're all manic depressives. At the moment I'm Happy, he's Grumpy,
he's Happy, so's he, those two are Grumpy, and he's Happy.'

Simon Meyrick-Jones, 1992

'I hope the children
aren't bothering you.'

Martin Honeysett, 1983

**WEST BIGGLESBY HEALTH AUTHORITY**
**£1,075,967.37**
**RECORD DAMAGES!**

Pete Dredge, 1991

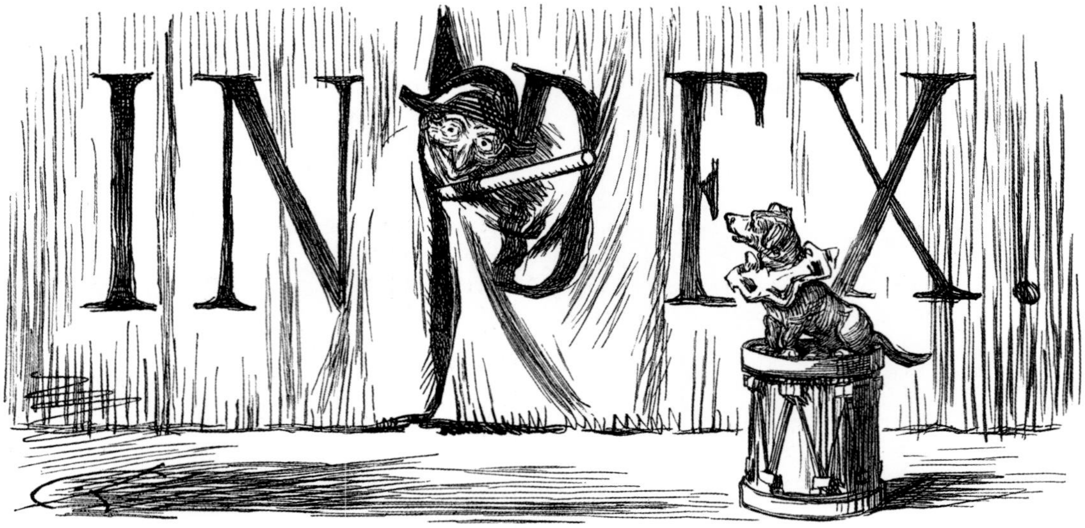
INDEX



Feature pages in **bold**

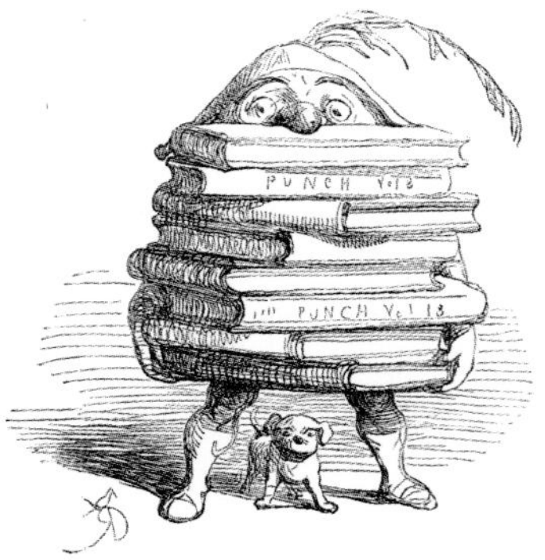
PUNCH Vol 18